ALL YOU WANTED TO KNOW ABOUT
Palmistry

VIJAYA KUMAR

New Dawn

NEW DAWN

An imprint of Sterling Publishers (P) Ltd.
A-59, Okhla Industrial Area, Phase-II,
New Delhi-110020.
Tel: 26387070, 26386209
Fax: 91-11-26383788: E-mail: sterlingpublishers@airtelmail.in
ghai@nde.vsnl.net.in
www.sterlingpublishers.com

All You Wanted to Know About - Palmistry
© Sterling Publishers Private Limited
ISBN 978-81-207-2198-2
Reprint 2009

Printed and Published by Sterling Publishers Pvt. Ltd.,
New Delhi-110 020.

Contents

	Preface	4
	Introduction	5
1.	Basic Characteristics	6
2.	Types of Hands	9
3.	The Fingers	16
4.	The Shape of Fingers	18
5.	The Form and Length	24
6.	Space between Fingers	28
7.	The Phalanges	30
8.	The Nails	33
9.	The Mounts	39
10.	The Planets	41
11.	The Lines	56
12.	Signs	137

Preface

This book is by no means an extensive study by any professional. The data provided in this book are my own interpretations of the subject, gleaned from various books, and presented from a layperson's viewpoint.

The book deals with each aspect of the study, point by point, in a simple language, and serves as a ready reckoner for those who have no time to go through heavy, indepth studies.

The publishers and I hold no responsibility for any discrepancy in the script. We would welcome suggestions or intimation of errors that come to anybody's notice.

Vijaya Kumar

Introduction

Palmistry, also known as Chirology, is a marvellous edifice today. It borrows its stones from the ancient civilisations of all lands.

Your palm is your personality. Very few people realise that they are carrying around a full-scape map of their character and potentialities.

Besides being a fascinating study, palmistry can help in vocational guidance, health and psychological diagnosis, partnership compatibility, etc.

Basic Characteristics

1. A person with hands often kept closed has a dark side to his character. He is probably a liar or a deceiver.
2. A person with fingers partially closed, and the hands hanging down naturally, is cautious and trustworthy.
3. An individual with fingers nearly open, and hands dangling at the sides, is credulous and mentally tardy.
4. Firmly closed fists, and hands at the sides, indicate a bully.

5. One whose hands are restless, moving up and down, in and out of pockets, is a man of strong character, but one who needs careful direction, since his emotions need to be controlled.

6. A person, moving his hands about, as though trying to keep them from touching anything, is suspicious, exceedingly watchful and cautious.

7. A subject, toying with some article or object, is excited about something.

8. Hands clasped in front indicates a person's calm and quiet temperament.

9. A person, rubbing his hands together as if washing them, is the personification of insincerity.

10. Limp, heavy hands by the sides indicate coarseness in a person and lack of sensitivity.

11. A person, clasping his hands behind him, is extremely cautious and indecisive.

Types of Hands

A) The Elementary Hand

1. Stiff, heavy, short fingers.
2. A short, clumsy thumb.
3. A thick, hard, square palm.
4. Shapeless fingertips.
5. Rough and leathery skin.

Characteristic Traits: Lack of enthusiasm and imagination; indifference to everything other than essential requirements, cowardly and violent when enraged.

Profession: Mostly labourers, boxers and wrestlers.

B) The Square Hand

1. A square palm.
2. A square wrist.
3. Square fingertips.
4. Knotty fingers.
5. A large thumb.
6. A square finger-base.

Characteristic Traits : Perseverance, foresight, truth, conventionality, love of order, fair play, reliability, discipline, down-to-earth, little imagination.

Profession: Usually businessmen, executives, lawyers, doctors, scientists and engineers.

C) The Spatulate Hand

1. A large thumb
2. Nailed phalanges flattened like a spatula.
3. Palms extremely broad near the base and tapering towards the base of the fingers, or vice versa.
4. Hands either soft and flabby, or firm and hard.

Characteristic Traits: Love of originality, invention and discovery, restless and excitable nature, energetic, purposeful, enthusiastic, valiant, industrious, active and dexterous.

Profession: Mostly artisans, craftsmen, inventors, explorers, navigators, pilots, astronauts, and engineers.

D) The Philosophic Hand
1. A long and angular hand.
2. Bony fingers.
3. Knotty joints.
4. A large, bony palm.
5. Nailed phalanges, half conical and half square.

Characteristic Traits: Calculative powers, the instinct of metaphysics, philanthropic in thought, psychic, dynamic, secretive, restless, careful in little matters, gifted with analytical powers.

Profession: Mostly philosophers, sages, poets, preachers, writers.

E) The Conical Hand
1. Smooth fingers.
2. Nails like cones.
3. A broad, thick and large palm.
4. A large thumb.

Characteristic Traits: Artistic skills, adaptability, short temper, generosity, intuitive power, love of change and variety, sensual pleasures, glamour, innovative skills, superb communicative skills, an ideal companion, wealth and fame, lack of prudence and foresight, an impulsive nature.

Profession: Painters, sculptors, poets, musicians, judges, and public relation officers.

F) The Psychic Hand

1. A small and slender hand
2. A medium palm.
3. Smooth fingers.
4. Long and tapering nailed phalanges.
5. A small and elegant thumb.

Characteristic Traits: A visionary and dreamy nature, insecurity, love of occult sciences lack of logic, discipline, order and punctuality.

Profession: Occultists.

The Fingers

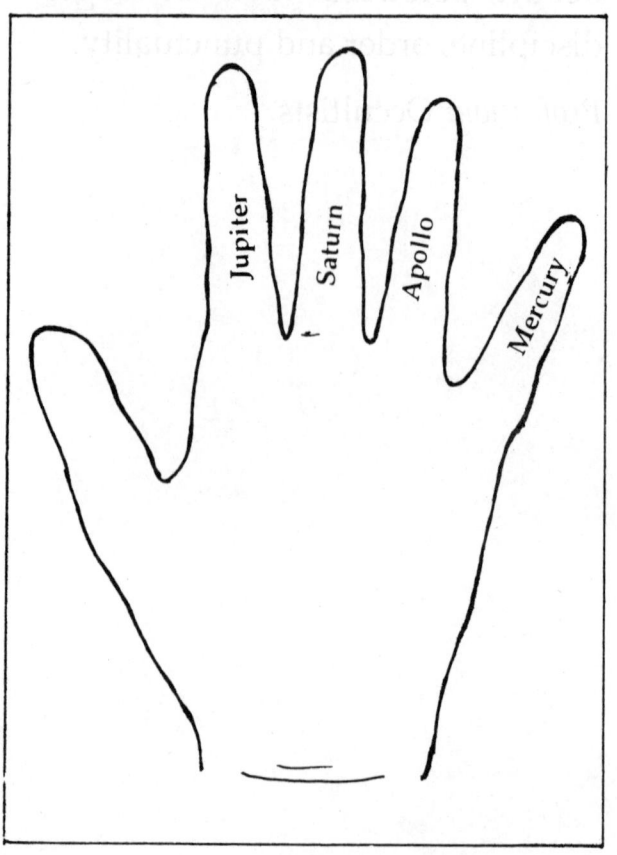

Planets Associated with Fingers

1. The *little finger*—Mercury—reveals health and professional ability.
2. The *ring finger*—Apollo—shows fame and fortune.
3. The *middle finger*—Saturn—indicates distinction and excellence.
4. The *index finger*—Jupiter—symbolises ambition and self-esteem.
5. The *thumb* shows power and authority.

The Shape of Fingers

A) Pointed

1. The person is cautious, intelligent and adaptable to situations.
2. He is a gifted conversationalist, and excels as a sales person or a PRO.
3. As an intellectual visionary, he has a leaning towards spiritualism.
4. Such a person is greatly attracted to the aesthetic, and is endowed with inspirational ideas.
5. Normally he struggles between inspiration and reasoning.

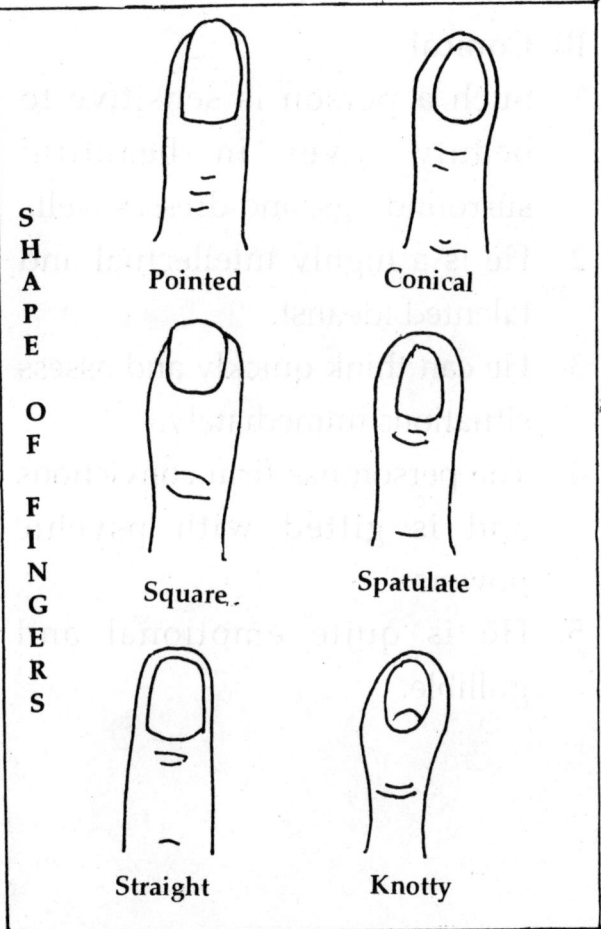

SHAPE OF FINGERS

Pointed   Conical

Square   Spatulate

Straight   Knotty

B) Conical

1. Such a person is sensitive to beauty, lives in beautiful surroundings, and dresses well.
2. He is a highly intellectual and talented idealist.
3. He can think quickly and assess situations immediately.
4. The person has firm convictions and is gifted with psychic powers.
5. He is quite emotional and gullible.

C) Square

1. This person has a talent for conceiving business plans, and loves reasoning.
2. He is a down-to-earth, practical person.
3. The person is tradition-bound and conforms to the social customs and legalities.
4. He is methodical and systematic.
5. For him, it is duty before anything else.
6. Such a person is an excellent financier.

D) Spatulate

1. The person is a pragmatic individual with a realistic approach.
2. He has a taste for travel and outdoor life.
3. Such a person is an achiever and is constantly on the move.
4. He is deeply involved in his professional activities.
5. Quite dynamic, creative and energetic.

E). Straight

1. Such a person is candid, forthright and gullible.

2. He is diligent, energetic and impulsive.
3. He always has harmony of thought and speech.
4. He is a great achiever.

F). Knotty
1. Such a person is calculative in the moves he makes.
2. Such a person lacks spontaneity.
3. His will-power and intellect are not in harmony.

The Form and Length

A) Long Fingers

1. Such a person is impulsive, hasty in judgement, and impatient.
2. He lacks conceptualisation, but is a great implementer.
3. The person can be selfish and cruel in his self-interest.
4. Some are overtly fond of food, drink and recreation.

B) Thick

1. The person is reliable and trustworthy.

2. He is materialistic and enjoys worldly pleasures.

C) Thin

1. Love of beauty and culture engross such a person's interest.
2. Diplomatic and in control of his emotions.
3. He is very careful and cautious, deliberating over decisions to be taken.
4. His evaluation skills are intensive.
5. Usually kind, helpful, and sympathetic, he is suspicious too.

D) Flexible

1. The person is cowardly, selfish and suspicious, especially indicated in a person with fingers bent towards the palm.

2. He is a good conversationalist, jovial, and a blurter of secrets.

E) Knotty

1. The person is analytical, with an eye for detail.

2. The first knots indicate cautiousness and carefulness in everything.

3. The second knots indicate an orderly mind.

4. When both knots are developed, the person can be quite a pain in the neck and difficult to live with.
5. When the third joints of the knuckles are uneven, negligence about cleanliness, health and punctuality is indicated.

F) Smooth
1. The person is given to impulse and rash judgements.
2. Quite emotional and ruled by passion.

Space between Fingers

1. A wide space between the thumb and the index finger—independent, generous, chaffes under restraint.
2. A space between the index and middle finger—disregard for conventions, forms his own opinions and not bound by others' opinions.
3. A space between the middle and ring finger—a harmonious balance between social needs and solitude.

4. A space between the ring and little finger—forthrightness, frankness, not bothered of what others think about him.

5. Spaces between all the fingers indicate a bohemian person who acts as he wishes, breaking conventions and traditions.

The Phalanges

1. When the first phalanx is longer— the person is governed by higher instincts.
2. When the second phalanx is longer— he is quite business-minded.
3. When the third phalanx is longer— he is interested in day-to-day living only.
4. Long phalanges—power and authority, ambition, patience and prudence.

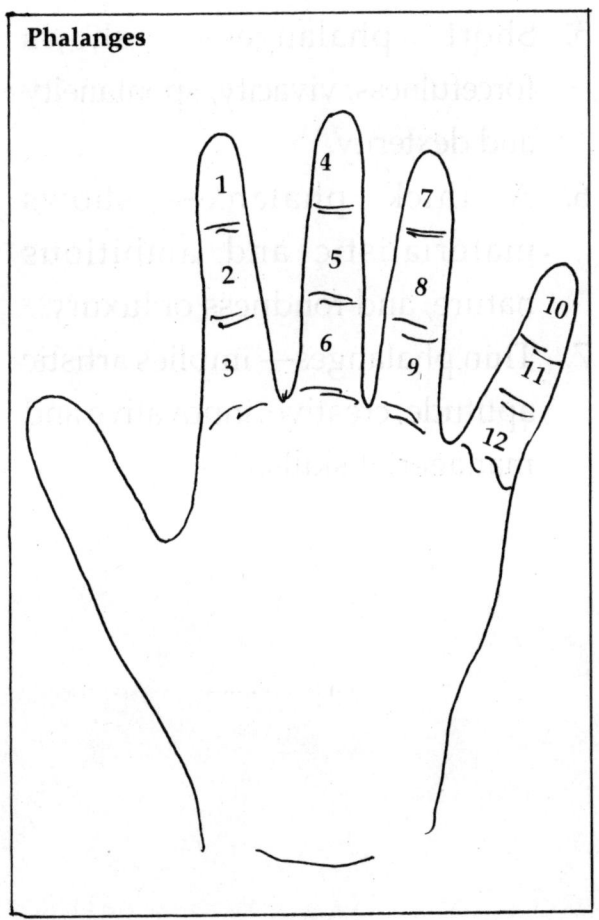

Phalanges

5. Short phalanges— shows forcefulness, vivacity, spontaneity and dexterity.
6. A thick phalanx— shows materialistic and ambitious nature, and fondness of luxury.
7. Thin phalanges— implies artistic aptitude, creative, innovative and managerial skills.

The Nails

A) Long
1. Long, thin, brittle—a weak physique.
2. Long, thin, curved—a violent disposition in love.
3. Long, thin, narrow—timidity and cowardice.
4. Long, broad, round—sound judgement.
5. Long, curved, thick—cruel and immoral.
6. Long, pink, sharp—good health, artistic tastes and emotional stability.

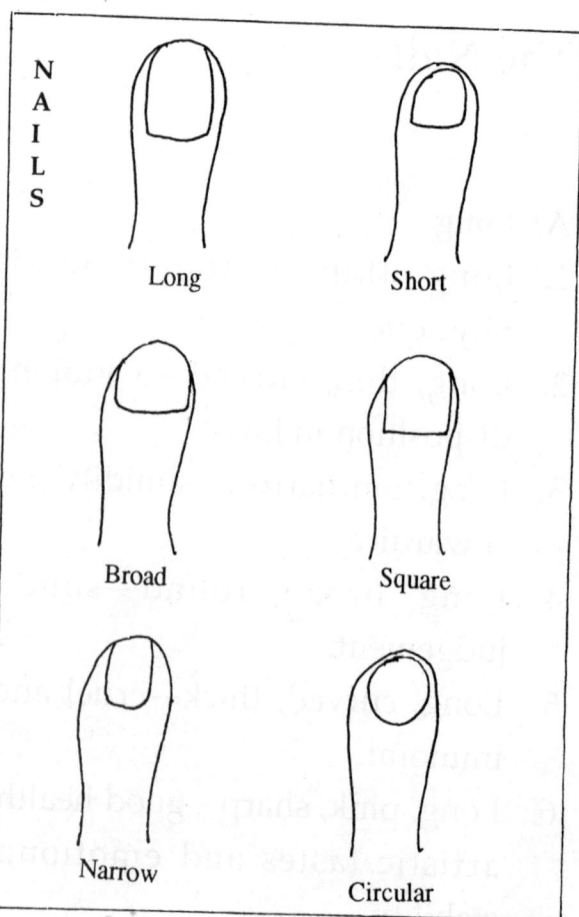

NAILS

Long

Short

Broad

Square

Narrow

Circular

7. Long, wide at the top, bluish at the base—afflictions of the heart.

8. Long with large moons—excessive blood circulation.

B) Short

1. Short, flat, shell-shaped—indicates sure signs of paralysis.

2. Short, flat, sunken into the flesh—nerve afflictions and paralytic tendencies.

3. Short, moonless—poor blood circulation.

4. Short, hard—a quarrelsome disposition.

5. Short, with a soft palm—an inborn critic.

6. Short, pale—deceitful and a weak character.

7. Short, red—a violent nature.

8. Short, square, bluish—heart problems.

9. Short, triangular—paralytic tendencies.

10. Short, narrow, curved—spinal trouble.

C) Broad

1. Broad, short—love of arguments and controversies.

2. Broad, medium—obstinacy.

3. Broad, square at the base—frankness, simplicity, optimism, self-confidence, a good temperament.

4. Broad, hard—volatility, good stamina.

D) Thin
1. Thin, very small—weak health, lack of vitality.
2. Thin nails, white spots—high-strung, nervousness.
3. Thin, long, curved—a violent disposition.
4. Thin, medium, curved—timidity, cowardice.

E) Square
1. Square, medium—aggressive, outgoing.
2. Square, long—realistic, diligent, trustworthy.

F) Narrow

1. Narrow, medium—gains through diplomacy.
2. Narrow, soft—a weak constitution.
3. Narrow, thin—narrow outlook, prone to nervousness and obstinacy.

G) Circular

1. Circular, medium—courage.
2. Circular, hard—hard-working, perseverance.
3. Circular, thin—capable of making quick decisions.

The Mounts

1. The fleshy pads at the base of the fingers and thumb are called mounts.
2. A raised mount with favourable signs on it shows it to be strong, while a flat mount with bad signs on it makes it weak.
3. An overdeveloped mount shows adverse qualities.
4. A triangle, a circle, or a vertical line on a mount are favourable signs.

5. A cross, a bar, a grille, an island, a dot, a horizontal line show some defects.

6. A pink hand, a square hand, or a spatulate tip of the finger shows an increase of the mount's strength.

7. A pointed or a conical finger decreases the power of the mount.

The Planets

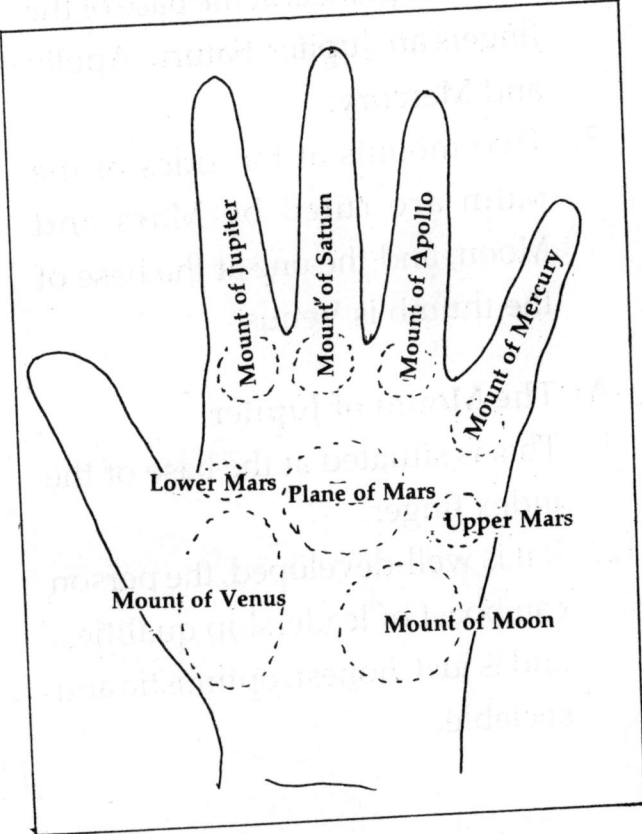

1. There are seven planets.
2. The four planets at the base of the fingers are Jupiter, Saturn, Apollo and Mercury.
3. Two mounts at the sides of the palm are ruled by Mars and Moon, and the one at the base of the thumb is Venus.

A) The Mount of Jupiter

1. This is situated at the base of the index finger.
2. If it is well-developed, the person can boast of leadership qualities, and is just, honest, optimistic and sociable.

Mount of Jupiter

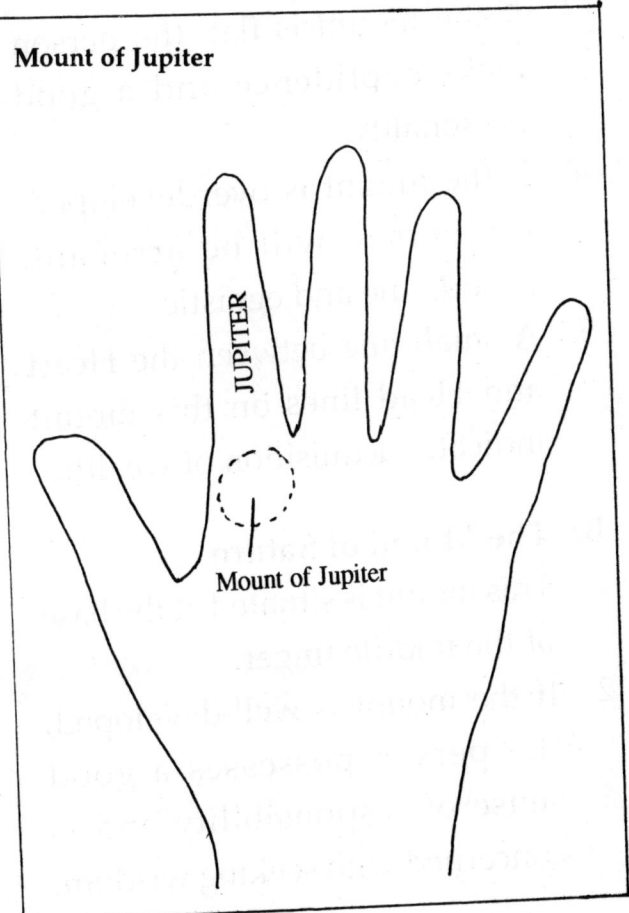

JUPITER

Mount of Jupiter

43

3. If the mount is flat, the person lacks confidence and a good personality.
4. If the mount is overdeveloped, the person will be arrogant, proud, idle and egoistic.
5. A small line between the Heart and Head lines on this mount indicates acquisition of wealth.

B) The Mount of Saturn

1. This mount is situated at the base of the middle finger.
2. If the mount is well-developed, the person possesses a good sense of responsibility and is concerned with seeking wisdom.

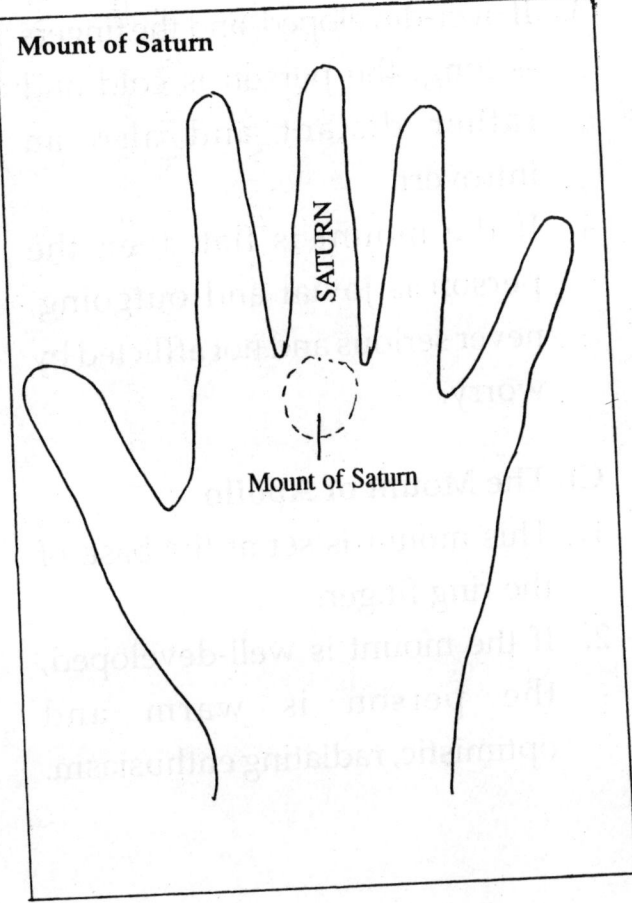

Mount of Saturn

SATURN

Mount of Saturn

3. If over-developed, and the fingers is long, the person is cold and rather distant and also an introvert.

4. If the mount is flat, then the person is jovial and outgoing, never serious and not afflicted by worry.

C) The Mount of Apollo

1. This mount is set at the base of the ring finger.

2. If the mount is well-developed, the person is warm and optimistic, radiating enthusiasm.

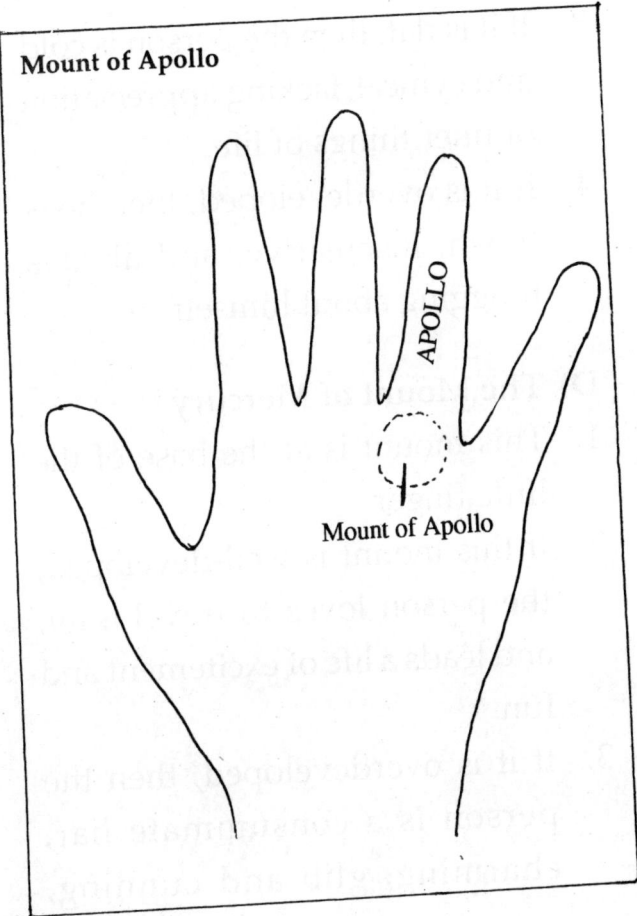

Mount of Apollo

APOLLO

Mount of Apollo

3. If it is flat, then the person is cold and cynical, lacking appreciation of finer things of life.

4. If it is overdeveloped, then he is brash, insensitive, and always bragging about himself.

D) The Mount of Mercury

1. This mount is at the base of the little finger.

2. If this mount is well-developed, the person loves to travel a lot, and leads a life of excitement and fun.

3. If it is overdeveloped, then the person is a consummate liar, charming, glib and cunning,

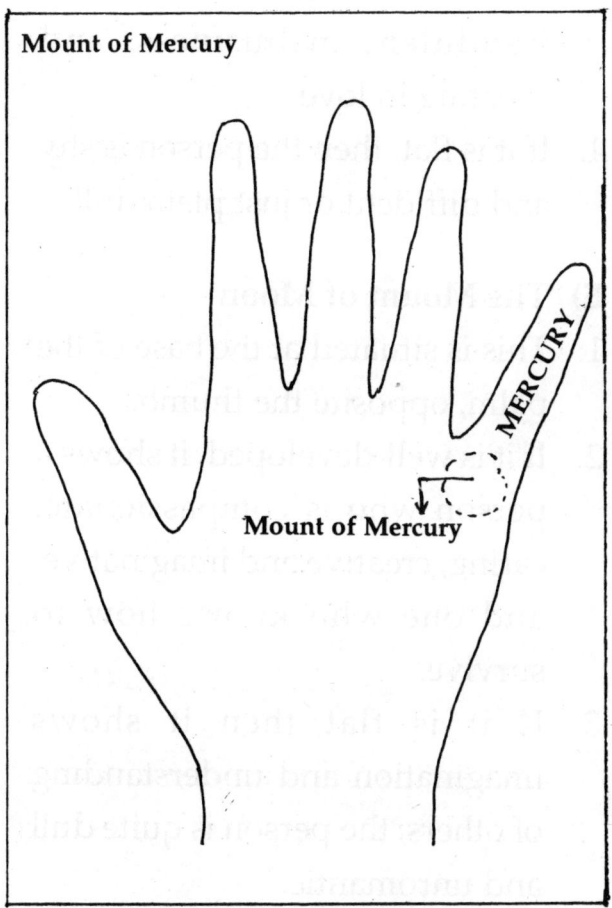

Mount of Mercury

Mount of Mercury

MERCURY

fraudulent in business, and cheating in love.

4. If it is flat, then the person is shy and diffident or just plain dull.

E) The Mount of Moon

1. This is situated at the base of the palm, opposite the thumb.

2. If it is well-developed, it shows a person who is compassionate, caring, creative and imaginative, and one who knows how to survive.

3. If it is flat then it shows imagination and understanding of others; the person is quite dull and unromantic.

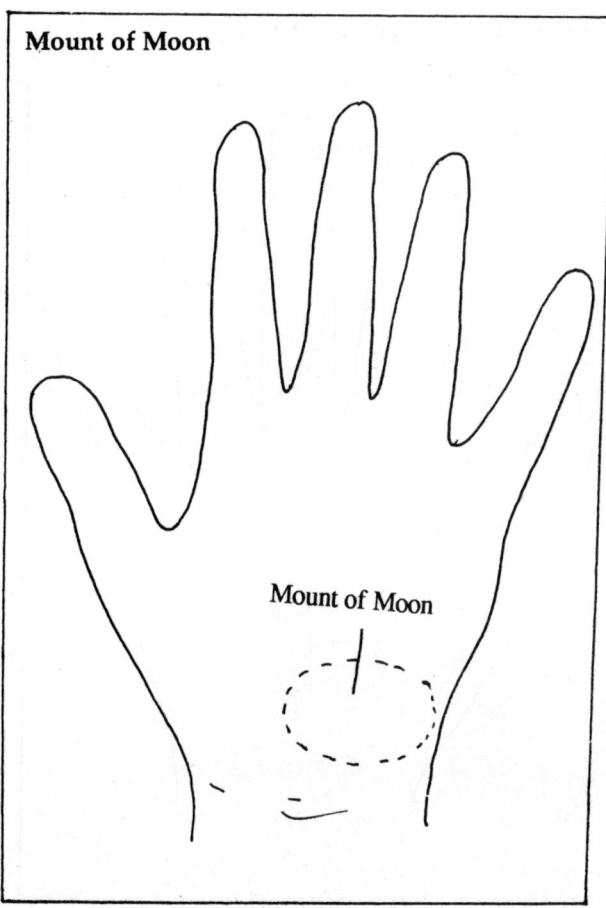

Mount of Moon

Mount of Moon

F) The Mount of Venus

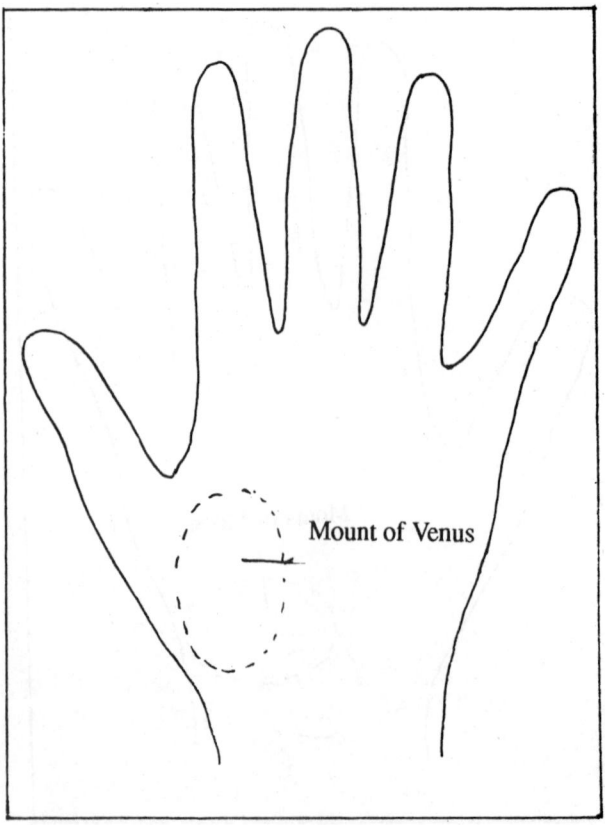

Mount of Venus

1. This is set under the thumb.
2. If the mount is well-developed, the person is warm and generous; he has much to offer in terms of companionship and social life, and sexually.
3. If it is over-developed, it shows one who is too greedy, intense, ambitious and fond of over-indulgence in worldly pleasures.
4. If it is flat, it shows lack of vitality and passion, and the person is cold and rather selfish, incapable of giving.

G) The Mount of Mars

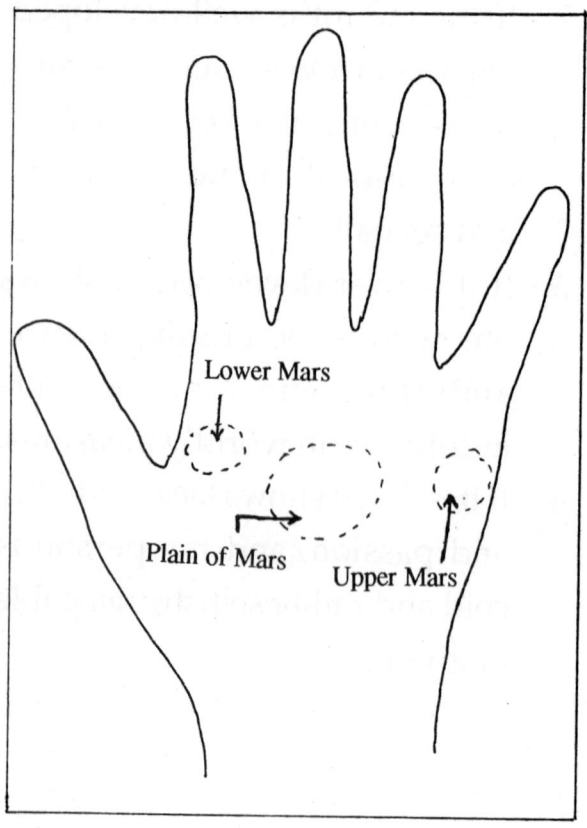

Lower Mars

Plain of Mars

Upper Mars

1. The Upper Mars lies between the Head line and the beginning of the Heart line.
2. The Lower Mars is near the thumb, at the beginning of the Heart line.
3. The Middle Mars (also called the Plane of Mars) is in the centre of the palm.
4. A very soft Plane of Mars shows a timid disposition.
5. A moderately thin and soft centre of the Plane of Mars shows self-centredness.
6. A thick, well-developed, and firm Plane of Mars shows abounding energy and joviality.

The Lines

A) The Life Line

1. This line starts between the thumb and the index finger, and goes to the wrist, curving widely around the thumb.
2. This line shows longevity, vitality, and quality of life.
3. An absent life line shows a person to be sluggish and high-strung.
4. A long and regular line indicates an excellent equilibrium, and a healthy constitution.

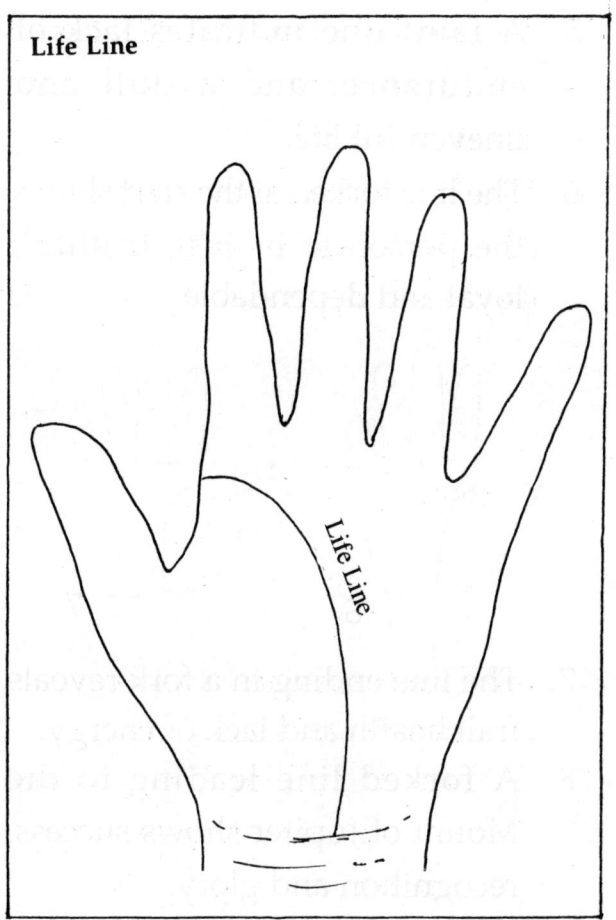

Life Line

Life Line

5. A faint line indicates lack of endurance, and a dull and uneventful life.

6. The line forked at the start shows the person to be just, truthful, loyal and dependable.

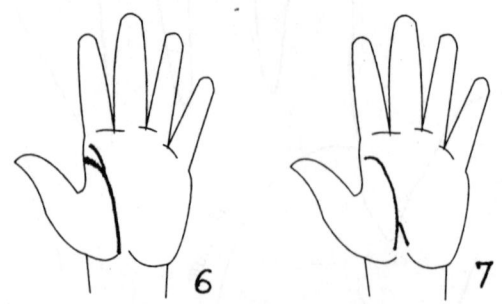

7. The line ending in a fork reveals frail health and lack of energy.

8. A forked line leading to the Mount of Jupiter shows success, recognition and glory.

9. A forked line going to the Mount of Moon indicates travel to distant places. If the line is faint, a miserable end follows; if deep, a comfortable end.

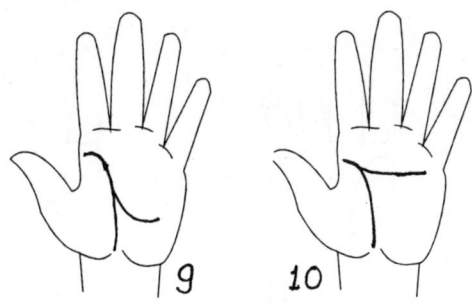

10. The line joining the Head line at the end of the index finger shows extreme caution, and lack of spontaneity.

11. The line starting on the Mount of Jupiter shows an ambitious person who takes excellent decisions, and has the ability to reach the top effortlessly.

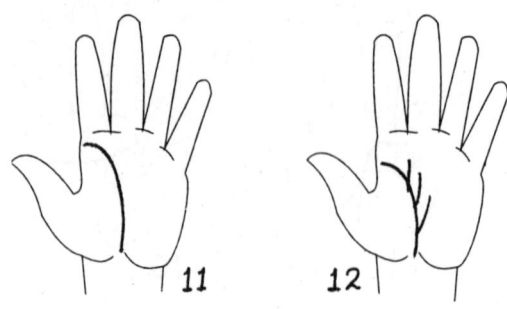

12. Branches rising upward show fortune, glory and success, achievements by sheer perseverance, and will-power.

13. Drooping branches indicate financial, social and emotional losses and disappointments.

14. A double line shows protection offered by a loved one, influence of the opposite sex, sexual impulses, and charged emotions.

15. A sister line reveals a healthy disposition, and a dynamic nature.

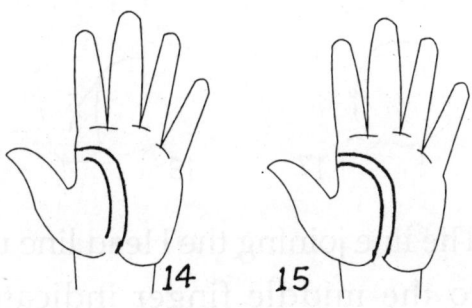

16. A long and faint line indicates a long life beset with health problems.

17. The line curving wide into the Mount of Moon indicates a very long life, indulgence in carnal pleasures, and an active imagination.

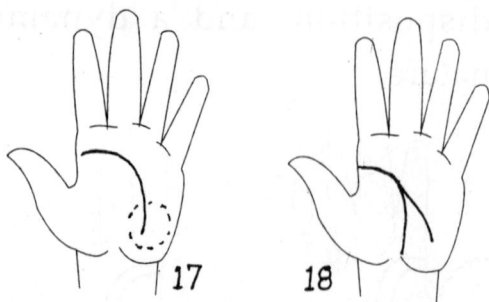

18. The line joining the Head line up to the middle finger indicates

caution, rational reasoning powers, and lack of confidence.

19. A long and deep line shows abundance of energy, and the person achieves his goal single-mindedly.

20. A faint, nearly straight line shows detachment from life.

21. Branches from the line leading to the Head line is indicative of wealth, vitality and success.

B) The Heart Line

1. This line runs horizontally on the upper palm, surrounding the Mounts of Mercury, Apollo and Saturn, and in some cases Jupiter also.

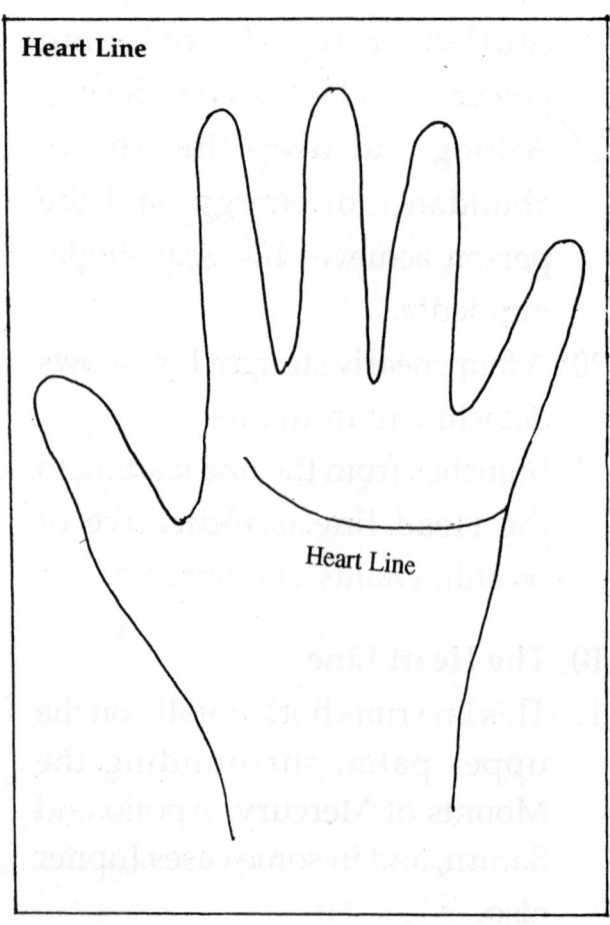

Heart Line

Heart Line

2. It rules emotions and relationships, and the person's generosity.
3. An absent line means that logic and reasoning are predominant, and the person uses any means to reach the top.
4. A long line shows an idealist in love.
5. A short line means that the individual sets importance to love of self.
6. An extremely long line, with the Heart line touching both sides of the palm, reveals limitless love, sensuality and lust, resulting in disastrous attachments.

7. One fork leading to the Mount of Saturn suggests that the person is ruled by passion and sensuality.

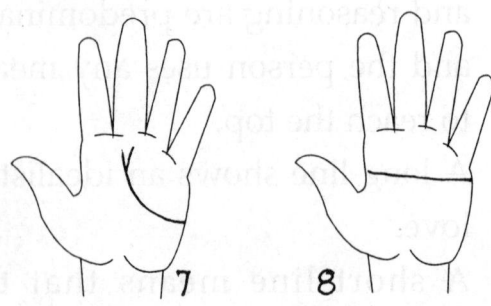

8. If it is straight and deep, running along the width of the palm, then jealousy, criminal tendencies, and insensitivity are indicated.

9. If it is clear and deep, then he is sincere, loyal, respectful, generous and considerate.

10. If it is set high, then indications of uncontrollable impulses, brutal tendencies, and calculative and ruthless traits are present.

11. One fork leading to the Mount of Jupiter and another to the Mount of Saturn show a fanatic rooted to ideals.

12. If it encircles the Mount of Mercury, then the person is gifted with occult powers.

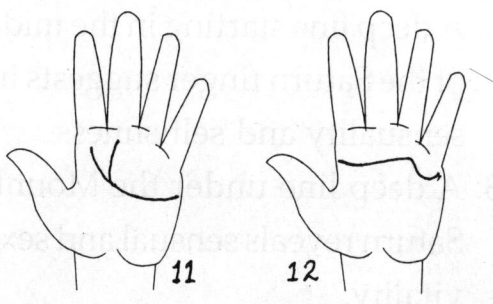

13. If it is low-set, then he is generous, kind and affectionate.
14. If the line is wavering, then he is unscrupulous, inconsistent and undependable.
15. Branches rising from the line indicate love and admiration from members of the opposite sex.
16. Drooping branches indicate betrayal from loved ones.
17. A deep line starting in the middle of the Saturn finger suggests lust, sensuality and selfishness.
18. A deep line under the Mount of Saturn reveals sensual and sexual vitality.

19. A poor line combined with a poor Head line shows lack of intelligence, a meddlesome trait, and a garrulous nature.

20. The line starting high on the Jupiter finger, combined with the Head and Life lines shows excessive love, thoughtlessness resulting in misfortune in love; and marriage in a high or wealthy family.

21. The line starting between the Mounts of Jupiter and Saturn reveals a dull life.

22. A deep line starting between the Mounts of Saturn and Jupiter

indicates intense love, high spiritual aspirations, and balanced emotions.

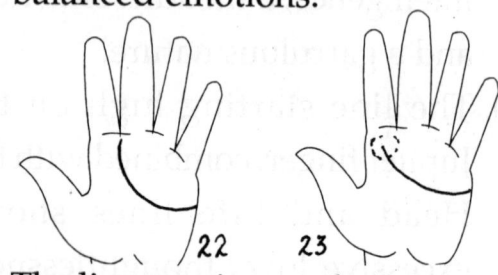

23. The line starting on the Mount of Jupiter shows a person to be honourable and reliable, and one who has realistic ideals.

24. A very deep line means a stressful life, and inability to handle emotions.

25. A very long line reaching the Mount of Jupiter indicates

intuition, philosophical bent of mind, generosity, love, passion and idealism.

26. One fork on the Mount of Jupiter and another towards the Head line, show self-deceit and deep hurt.

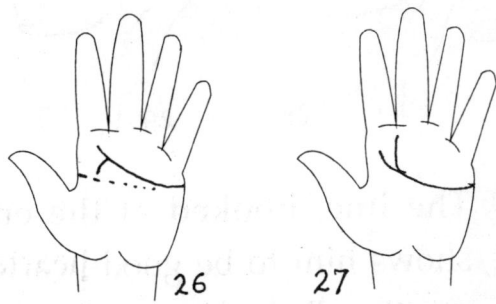

27. One fork on the Mount of Jupiter, and one between the index and middle fingers show harmony and love in domestic life.

28. A faint, long line from one side to the other shows the person to be proud and sensitive.

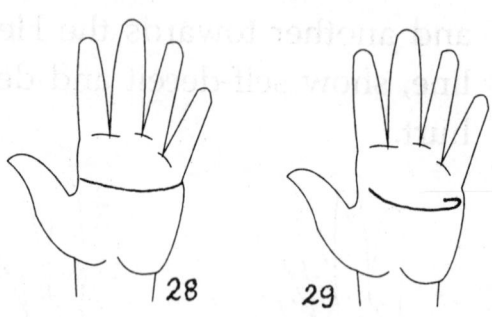

28   29

29. The line, hooked at the end, shows him to be good-hearted, emotionally insecure, jealous and suspicious.

30. If the Heart line touches the Head line and the Life line, then the

person suffers deeply due to betrayal of love.

31. One fork towards the Head line and another to the Mount of Moon shows him given to wild imaginations, resulting in sorrow.

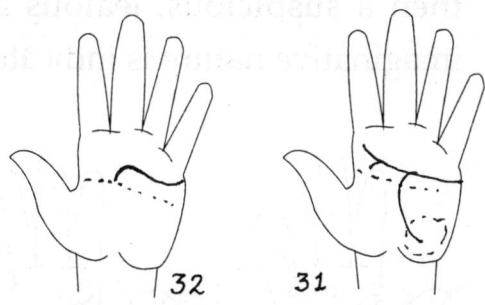

32   31

32. If it joins the Head line under the Mount of Saturn, disastrous disappointments from his

beloved due to unrealistic adoration are indicated.

33. If it is intertwined with the Head line at the start, then the person is very ambitious, reaching the goal at the cost of others.

34. If it slopes to the Mount of Moon, then a suspicious, jealous and imaginative nature is indicated.

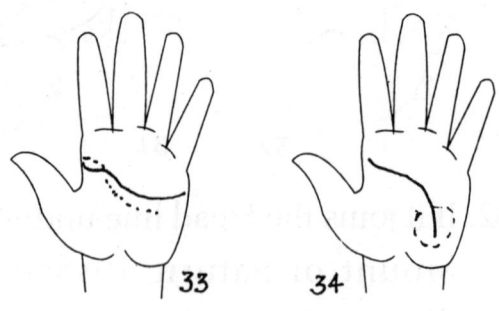

33   34

35. If it is short and faint, it indicates a fleeting relationship.
36. A very deep line under the middle finger shows a loner with a strained heart.
37. If it curves towards the Head line, then the person is interested in intellectual pursuits.

C) The Head Line
1. This runs horizontally in the middle of the palm below the Heart line.
2. It rules memory, intelligence, perceptions, reasoning and concentration powers.

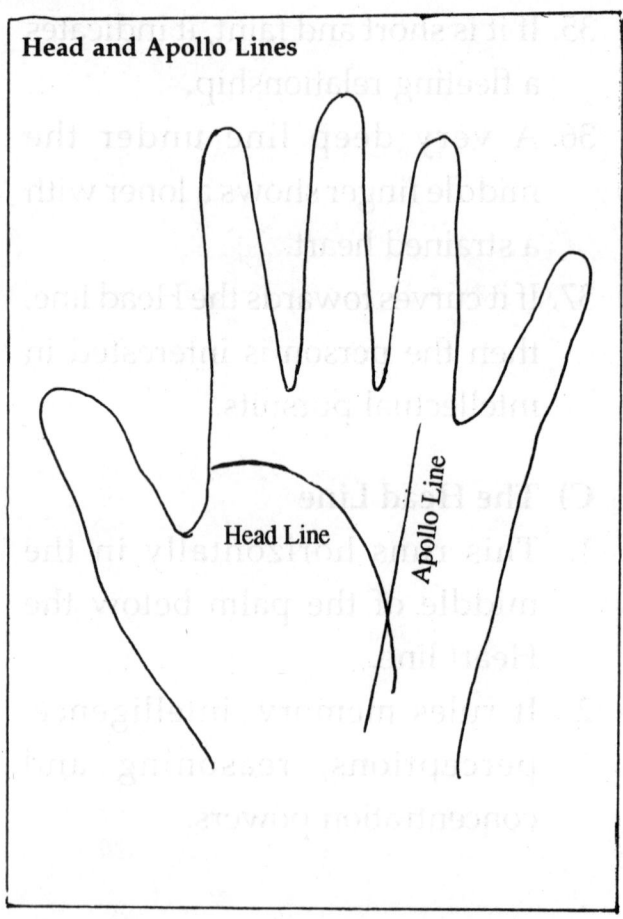

Head and Apollo Lines

Head Line

Apollo Line

3. A short line indicates perception and intuitive capabilities.
4. A straight line suggests intelligence, practicality and materialism.
5. The line, curving to the Mount of Moon, shows the person to be imaginative and creative.
6. An absent line shows simple-mindedness, submissiveness, lethargy, and sometimes insanity.
7. If it is separated from the Life line, then the person is independent, self-reliant, impulsive and unpredictable.
8. A long and straight line shows forthrightness, outspokenness,

ambitions, practicality, and an excellent memory.

9. If it is long and straight, splitting the palm in half, the person is sadistic, abusive, cruel and brutal.

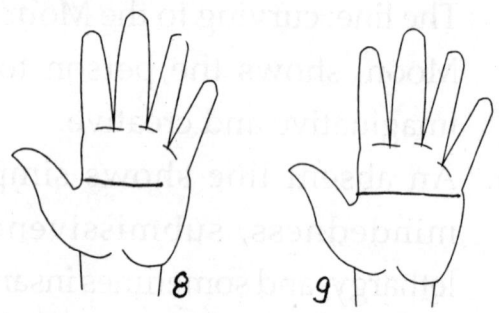

10. A long, straight and faint line shows narrow-mindedness and intolerance.

11. A short and curved line shows creativity and strong instincts, but lack of firmness of character.

12. A double line reveals a highly gifted and talented person, with a flair for business.

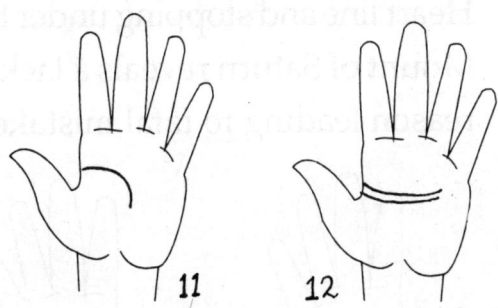

13. A short, deep and straight line ending on the Saturn finger indicates a person with limited views and lack of perception.

14. If it is short and faint, it indicates limited intelligence and poor memory.

15. Rising lines from the Head line to the Heart line shows gullibility.

16. The line curving towards the Heart line and stopping under the Mount of Saturn reveals a lack of reason leading to fatal mistakes.

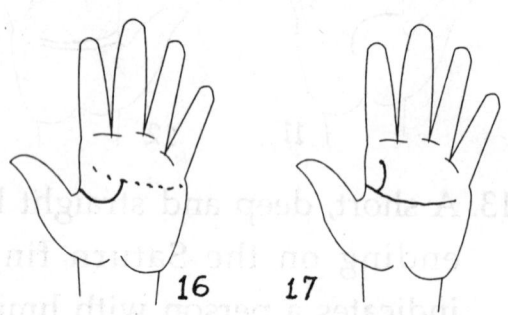

16   17

17. A fork towards the Mount of Jupiter shows recognition and contentment in professional life.

18. If it joins the Life line to form an acute angle, then the person is careful and discreet, discerning and discriminating.

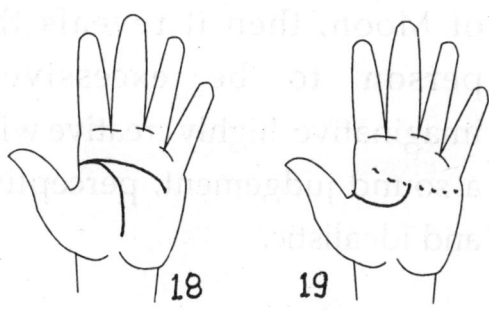

19. If it curves between the Apollo and Saturn fingers, but stops on the Heart line, then he is highly dependent, emotionally and materially, on another person.

20. If it slopes widely to the Rascette, then he is artistic, creative, and interested in occult sciences.

21. If it slopes widely to the Mount of Moon, then it reveals the person to be excessively imaginative, highly creative with a sound judgement, perceptive and idealistic.

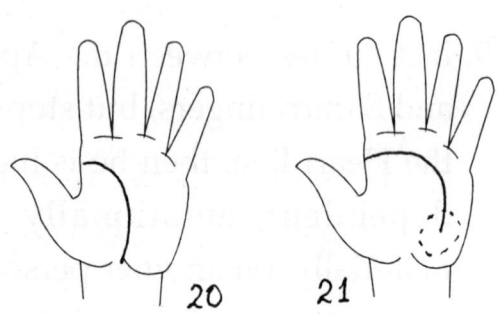

22. If it joins the Life line up to the Saturn finger, then inability to take decisions independently, cautiousness and lack of confidence are revealed.

23. The line starting under the Mount of Saturn indicates great unhappiness due to conceit, stubbornness and rashness.

24. The line, slightly separated from the Life line, shows a pleasant and enthusiastic person with a sound judgement.

25. With forks going to the Mount of Moon, the person is melancholic and morbid.

26. One fork towards the Heart line indicates passion and emotions concerning a loved one which leads to ruin.

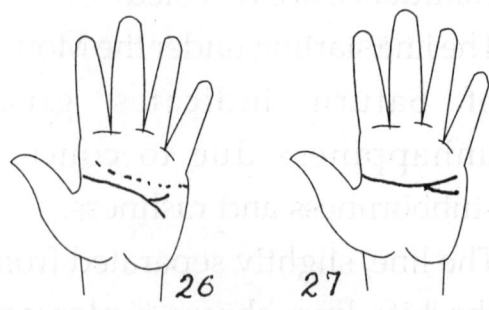

27. The line ending in a fork of equal length reveals a well-balanced, perceptive and creative person.

28. A knotty line shows violent and murderous instincts, and problems from chronic neuralgia.

29. The line, starting from the Heart line, shows that his feelings are ruled by reason rather than logic.

30. The line, starting inside the Jupiter finger, shows extreme self-confidence, conceit, extravagance, vainglory and rashness.

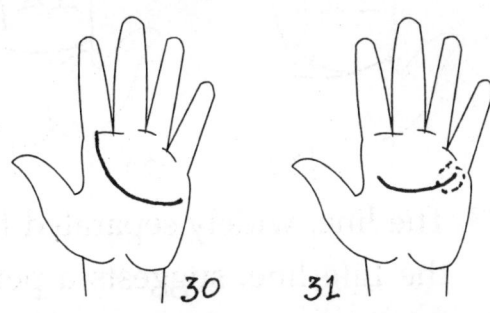

31. The line ending on the Mount of Mercury shows a calculating, shrewd, deceptive and dishonest person.

32. A fork to the Mount of Mercury shows an ambitious person with an excellent command over language, and hypnotic powers.

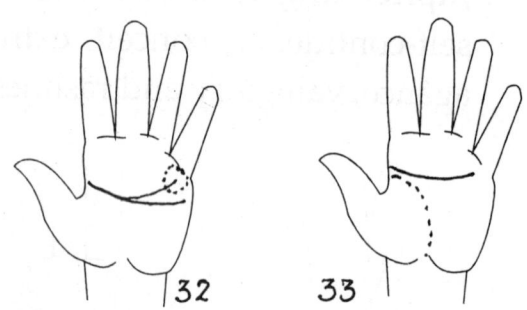

33. The line, widely separated from the Life line, suggests a person who is impulsive, rash, self-confident, hysterical at times, and an independent thinker.

34. Rising branches from the line show high aspirations without focus.

35. Drooping branches indicate constant griefs and disappointments.

36. A hooked line shows one to be cowardly, spineless, self-indulgent, and a traitor.

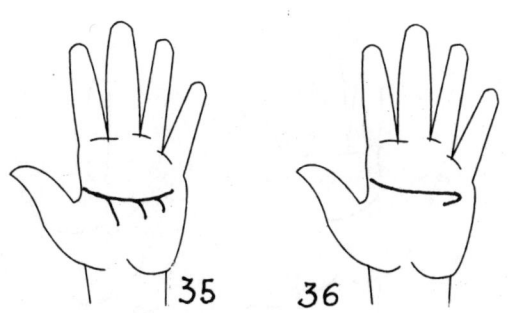

37. The line starting inside the Life line reveals an erratic, timid, anti-social and insecure person.

38. A short line shows him to be short-sighted, morose, and lacking in concentration.

39. If it curves between the Apollo and Mercury fingers, he is artistic, having commercial know-how.

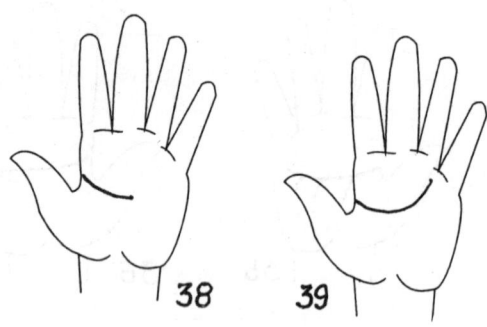

40. If it ends on the Mount of Apollo, then he is highly talented and artistic.

41. If it is setlow, then he is greedy and frugal.

42. A wavering line indicates deceit, falseness, purposelessness, and an unscrupulous quality.

43. If it is straight, with a fork leading to the Mount of Moon, then he is practical, imaginative and has exaggerating tendencies.

D) The Fate Line

1. This line rises from the base of the palm, and runs to the Mount of

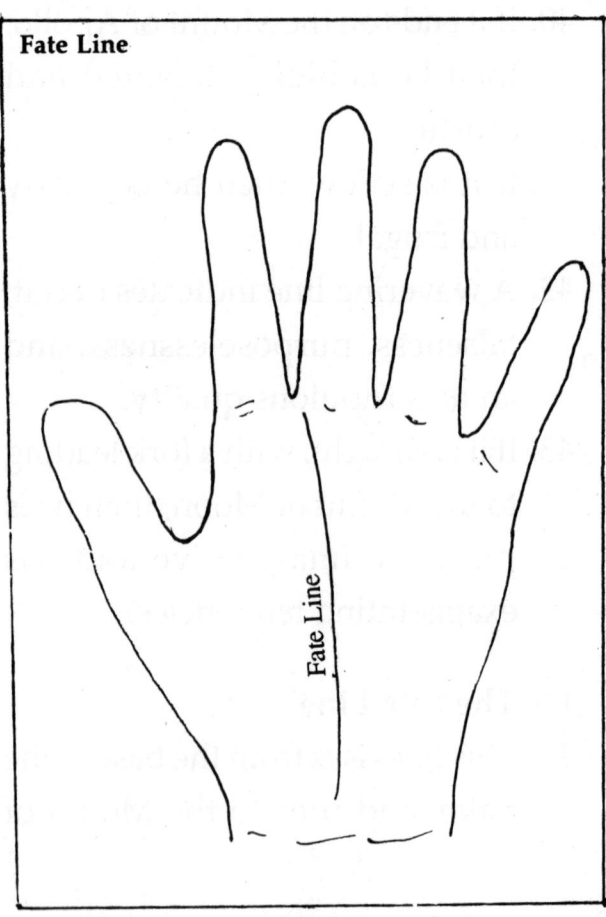

Fate Line

Saturn, dividing the palm into two halves.

2. An absent line shows that the man is self-made, diligent, leading an uneventful life.

3. One fork to the Mount of Apollo suggests celebrity and glory; he is talented, artistic with interests in music and literary pursuits.

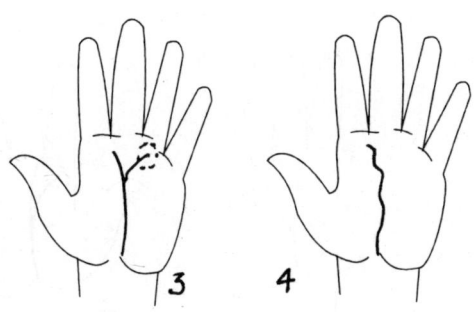

4. The line ending in a fork on the Mount of Saturn, shows a prudent, intellectual, discreet, distinguished and mysterious person.

5. One fork towards the Mount of Mercury suggests tremendous success in business, and a gift of persuasive powers.

6. A fork towards the Mount of

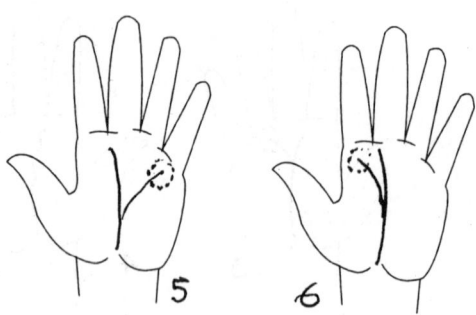

Jupiter shows leadership qualities leading to fame and fortune, diplomacy, a pleasant personality and a humanitarian approach.

7. If the line runs deep into the Saturn finger, then fame, fortune, travels and excellent health are indicated.

8. If it starts from the Mount of Moon, then success and affluence through help of friends are assured.

9. A fork at the start shows a traumatic childhood, affecting choice of career, but eventually success is guaranteed.

10. A double line protects one from adversities in life.

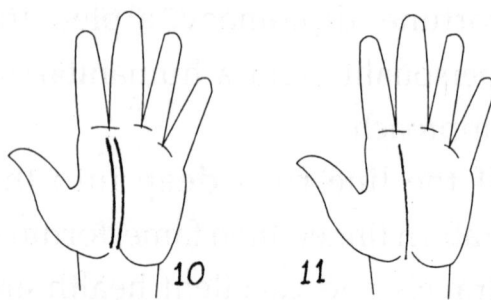

11. If it is a faint line, then indifference to surroundings, and missed opportunities to success is indicated.

12. If it starts from the Rascette, success is ensured right from childhood, with early responsibilities.

13. If it is malformed at first, childhood is traumatic; the person has a good sense of judgement, has a positive attitude, and will be prosperous in later years.

14. Branches touching the Fate line indicate heart-break which affects career and social status.

15. Rising branches indicate a successful career with great opportunities and prosperity.

16. Drooping lines mean heavy losses, failure, and disappointments in career.

17. A wavering line shows a person to be indecisive, lethargic, lacking

purpose, and indulging in worldly pleasures.

18. An unusually deep line reveals inheritance of family business, and success which is devoid of a sense of achievement.

E) The Line of Apollo

1. This line runs vertically from the base of the palm to the middle of the ring finger.

2. It indicates brilliance, fame, recognition, and a life of luxury.

3. An absent line indicates success only through hard-work and perseverance.

4. If it starts from the Mount of Mars, success is ensured through perseverance and discipline.
5. If it starts from the Mount of Venus, rise to fame due to the help of loved ones is indicated.

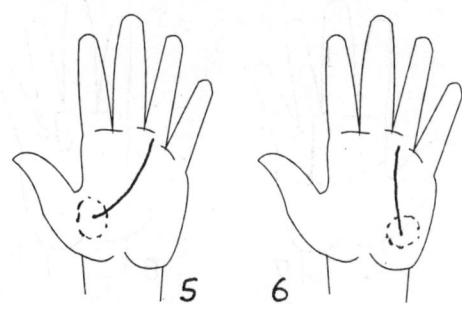

6. If it rises from the Mount of Moon, the person is extraordinarily imaginative, an excellent writer or composer, and creative and persuasive.

7. If it starts from the Head line, excellence in academic, and success in middle age through intellectual and creative abilities, are assured.

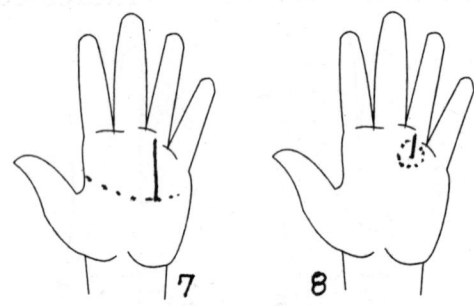

8. If the line is very small on its mount, success comes late in life.
9. If it is thick, notoriety is indicated.
10. A fork at the end suggests talents which have no focus.

11. Sister lines imply success and recognition without effort.

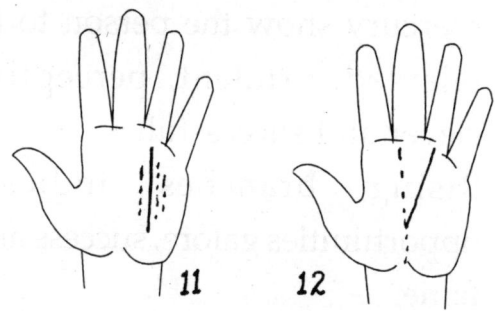

12. If it starts from the Fate line, the person achieves success and prosperity, and yet is deeply involved with his work.
13. If it starts from the line of Mercury, success is achieved effortlessly due to intutive powers.

14. One fork on the Mount of Saturn and another one on the Mount of Mercury show the person to be talented, prudent, perceptive clever and successful.

15. Rising branches indicate opportunities galore, success and fame.

16. Drooping branches are indicative of losses and disappointments.

17. If it starts from the Mount of Mars, success through perseverance and discipline are ensured.

18. If it is faint, there is negligible recognition and wealth.

19. If the line stops on the Head line, the talents of the person are not optimised.

20. If it starts from the Heart line, then success comes in later years through sheer hard work.

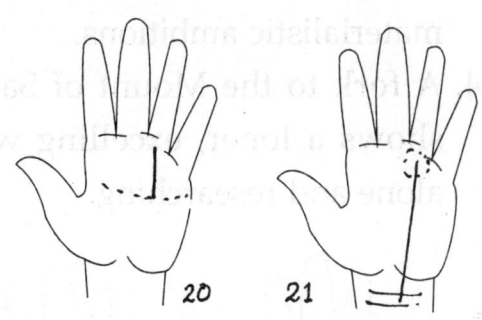

21. A clear, deep line from the Rascette to its own mount brings great fame, recognition, and success through aptitudes which makes a person arrogant.

22. A wavering line shows success to be elusive due to a wavering mind.
23. If it runs straight towards the Mount of Mercury, the person's talents are wasted due to materialistic ambitions.
24. A fork to the Mount of Saturn shows a loner, excelling when alone and researching.

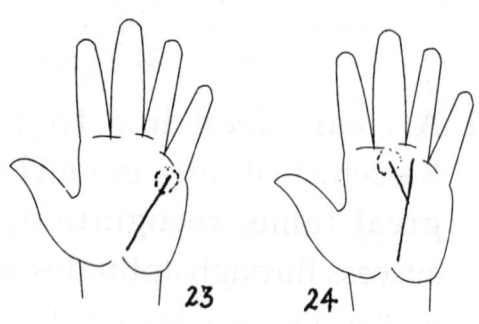

23   24

25. If it starts from the Fate line, it shows recognition and contentment, and commitment to work.

26. If it is long and faint, going straight to its mount, the person is very prosperous and yet humble and balanced.

F) The Line of Mercury

1. This line runs from the base of the palm to the Mount of Mercury.

2. It reveals the balance between body and mind.

3. An absent line shows an alert and shrewd mind.

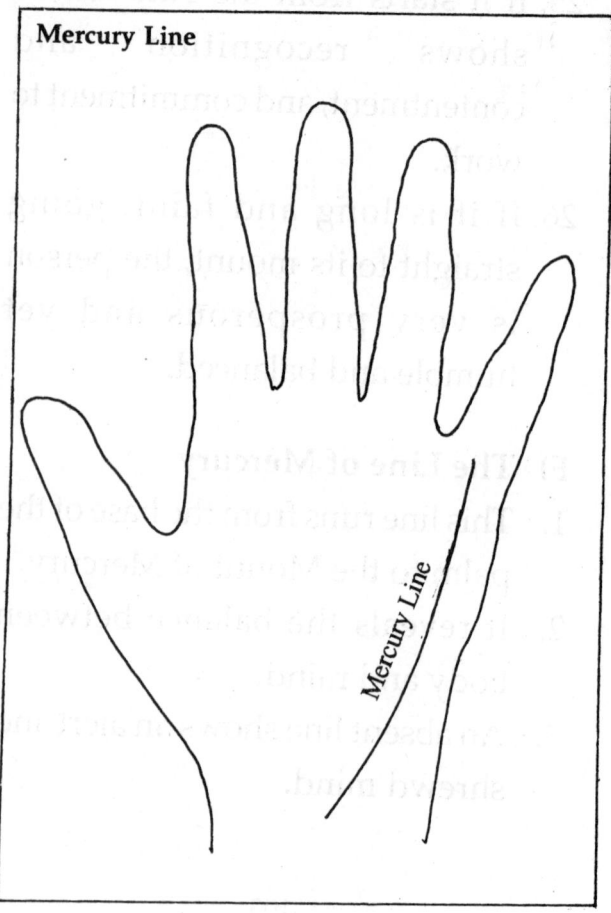

Mercury Line

Mercury Line

4. If it is faint, loss of wealth and status occur.
5. If it starts from the Life line, success is indicated through efforts; also good health.
6. If it starts from the Rascette, honour, success, and competence in business are indicated.

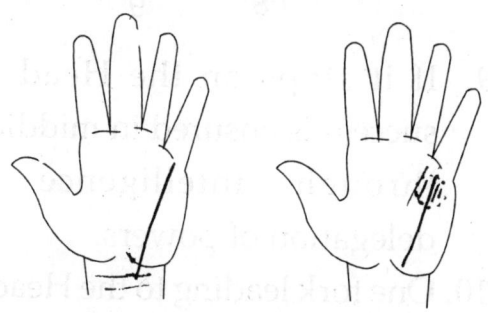

7. If it ends in parallel lines, lavish living during prosperous years ends in mediocrity in old age.

8. If it ends in a fork, productivity and achievements will be minimal.

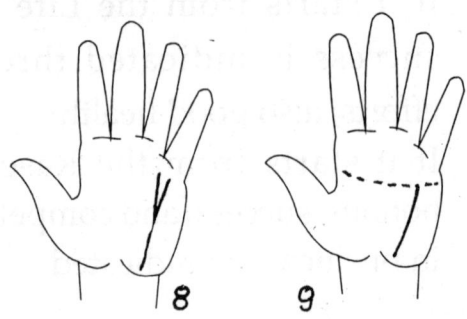

9. If it stops on the Head line, success is ensured in middle age through intelligence and delegation of powers.

10. One fork leading to the Head line indicates prosperity through mental efforts.

11. A poor line ending on the Heart line shows heart-related illnesses, as well as remaining single.
12. Drooping branches suggest extra efforts required to stay in business.
13. A fork to the Mount of Jupiter indicate leadership qualities leading to success.

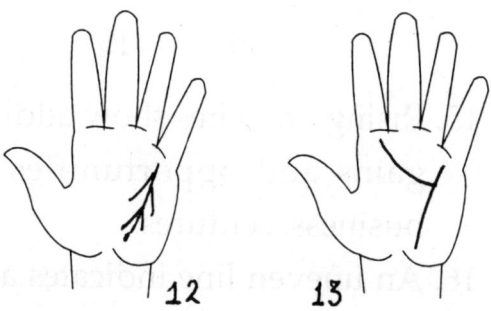

14. A fork to the Mount of Apollo shows a well-mannered, dignified, good-looking being with a magnetic personality who is successful in life.

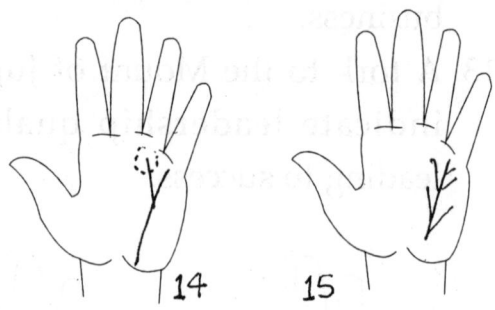

15. Rising branches show additional gains and opportunities from business ventures.

16. An uneven line indicates a cycle of waning and waxing successes.

17. A wavering line makes the person irritable, unstable, dull, with a weak memory.

18. If it starts from the Rascette and goes to the Mount of Apollo, then one can be sure of prosperity, fame and wealth.

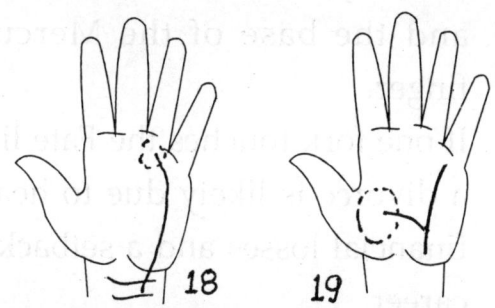

19. A fork to the Mount of Venus indicates help from a member of the opposite sex in business ventures.

20. A forked line shows conflicting interests hampering success.

G) The Line of Union

1. This Line rises from the edge of the palm towards the Mount of Mercury, between the Heart line and the base of the Mercury finger.

2. If one fork touches the Fate line, a divorce is likely due to heavy financial losses and a setback in career.

3. A fork to the line of Apollo brings fame and fortune leading to a good family life.

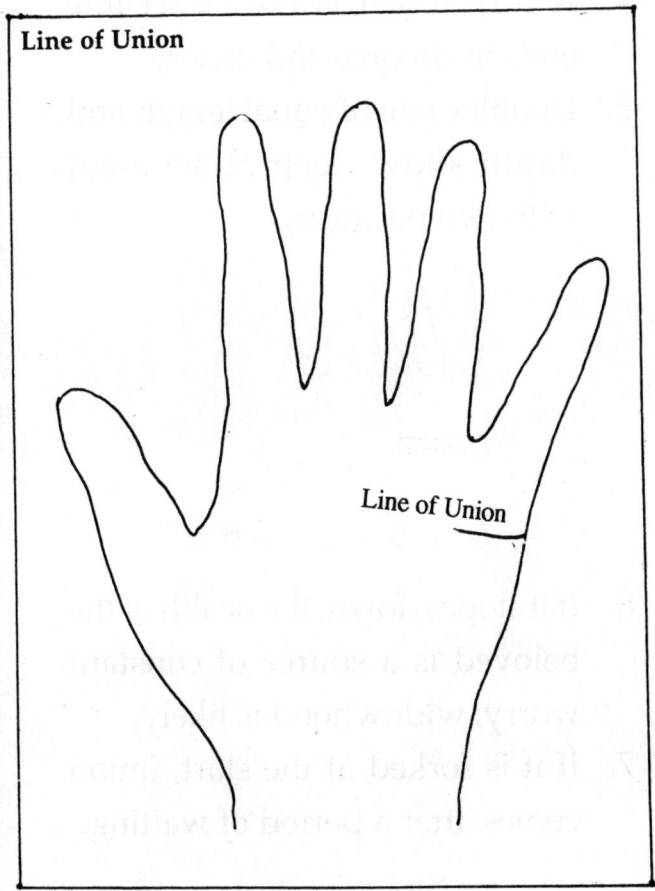

Line of Union

Line of Union

4. A fork towards the Heart line ends in divorce and misery.

5. Doubles line of equal length and depth show deep attachment with two partners.

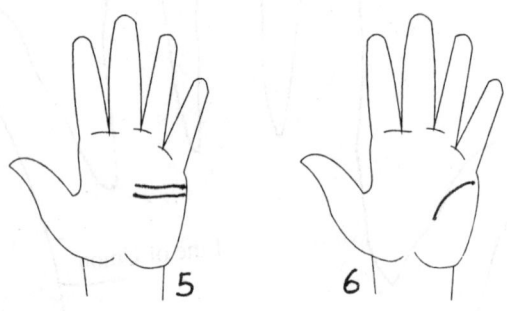

6. If it slopes down, the health of the beloved is a source of constant worry; widowhood is likely.

7. If it is forked at the start, union comes after a period of waiting.

8. If it is forked at the end, separation from the beloved might result due to personality clashes.

9. If it touches the line of Apollo, marriage with a rich and famous person brings the person into the limelight.

10. Several parallel lines show a fickle mind.

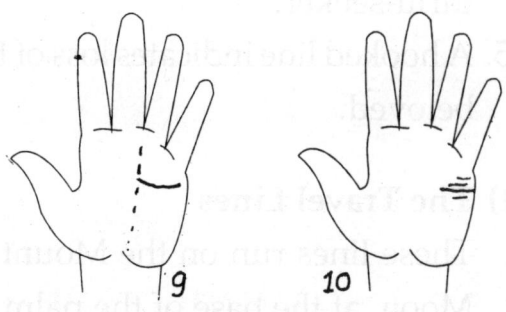

11. Drooping lines indicate disappointments, emotional drain, and betrayal.
12. Rising lines indicate a joyful and happy union.
13. A deep and short line shows profound love, passion and loyalty.
14. The line curving upwards shows a selfish nature, incapable of sharing; who is also a shallow thrill-seeker.
15. A hooked line indicates loss of the beloved.

H) The Travel Lines

1. These lines run on the Mount of Moon, at the base of the palm.

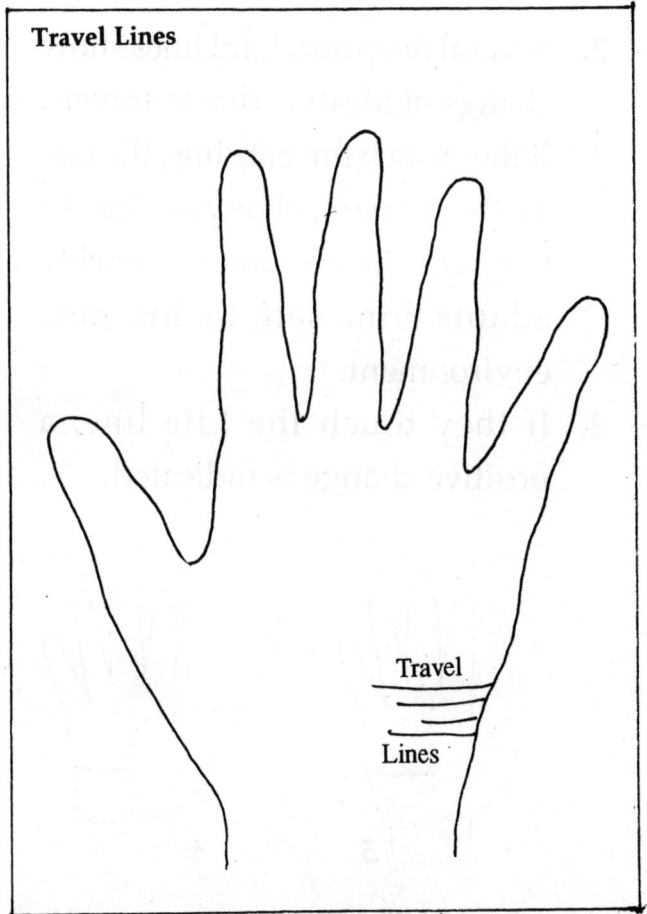

Travel Lines

Travel

Lines

2. Several deep and faint lines show change of lifestyle due to travels.
3. If they touch the Fate line, the fate of the person changes due to frequent travels, and he quickly adapts him self to his new environment.
4. If they touch the Life line, a positive change is indicated.

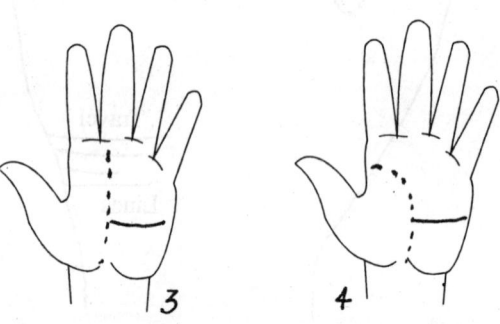

5. If a line crosses the Life line and ends on the Mount of Venus, the subject travels to be with a loved one.

6. If the lines are faint, frequent travels occur.

I) The Lines of Influence

1. These run from the Mounts of Venus, Upper and Lower Mars, vertically, horizontally or concentrically.

2. Horizontal lines are favourable.

3. If they start from the Mount of Venus and end on the Life line, influence by near ones, causing changes in life, is indicated.

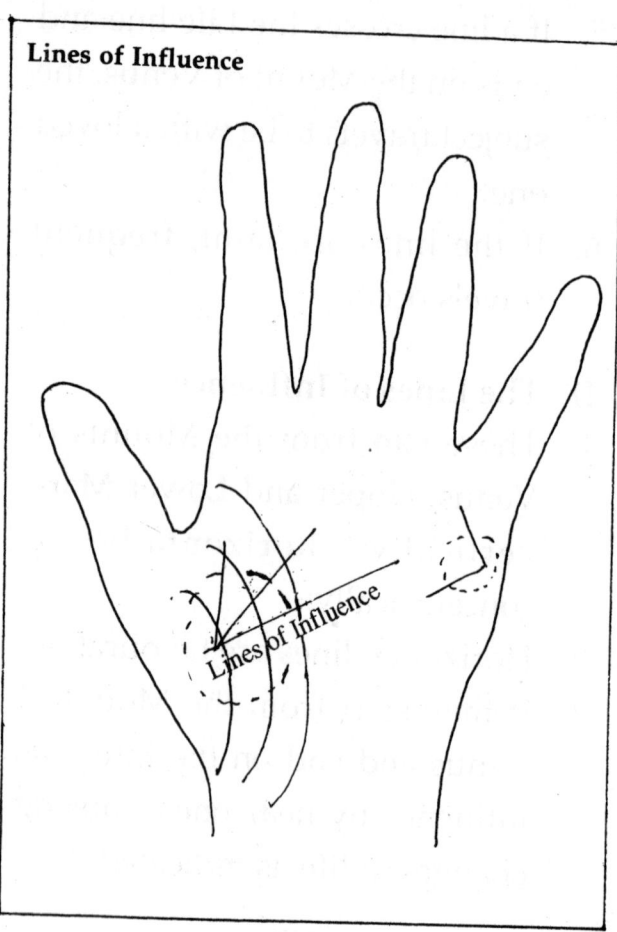

Lines of Influence

Lines of Influence

4. If they start from the Mount of Venus with a star and cross the Life line, there is grief due to the loss of a loved one.

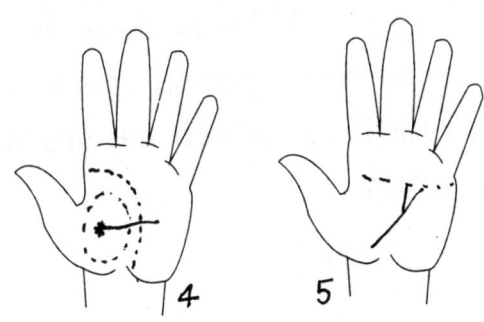

5. If a line ends in a fork on the Heart line, a heavy influence by a loved one, which can later cause a separation, is indicated.

6. If a line starts from the Mount of Venus and stops on the Head

line, the person is unable to act independently or decide quickly.

7. If it starts from the Mount of Venus and crosses the line of Union, there is deep hatred between the person's partner and relatives, which causes deep worry.

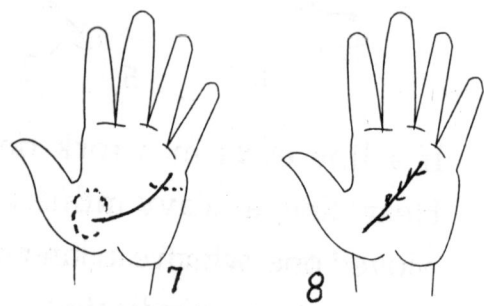

8. Capillary lines shows influence by one who is influenced by another.

9. If a line merges with the Fate line, the influence of a loved one strengthens the career and social status of the person.

10. If a line ends in a fork on the Heart line, the heavy influence of a lover ends in separation later.

11. If a line starts from the Mount of Venus and merges with the Life line at the start, the person will be highly influenced by one of the opposite sex, and become self-reliant later.

12. If a line starts from Upper Mars and stops on the Mount of Jupiter, influence of religious

beliefs or patriotic fervour is shown.

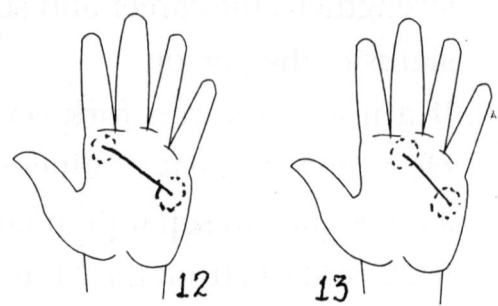

13. If it starts from Upper Mars and ends on the Mount of Saturn, occult sciences, black magic, telepathy, visionary power, etc., predominate.

14. If it starts from Upper Mars and ends on the Mount of Mercury, mercenary quatities are indicated.

J) The Lines of Mars

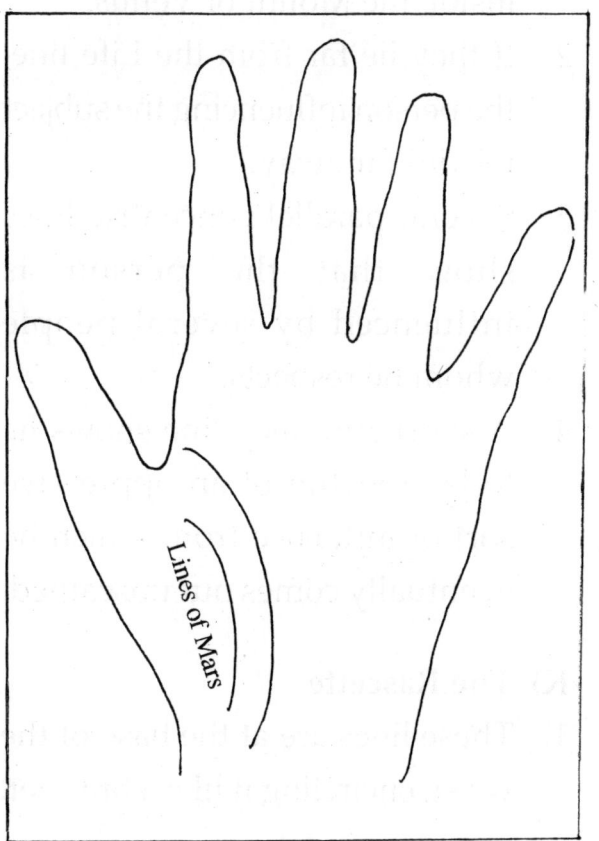

Lines of Mars

1. These are deep, concentric lines inside the Mount of Venus.
2. If they lie far from the Life line, the person influencing the subject resides far away.
3. Several parallel concentric lines show that the person is influenced by several people whom he respects.
4. A short and deep line shows he to be a victim of an oppressive sort of influence from which he eventually comes out unscathed.

K) The Rascette

1. These lines are at the base of the wrist, encircling it like a bracelet.

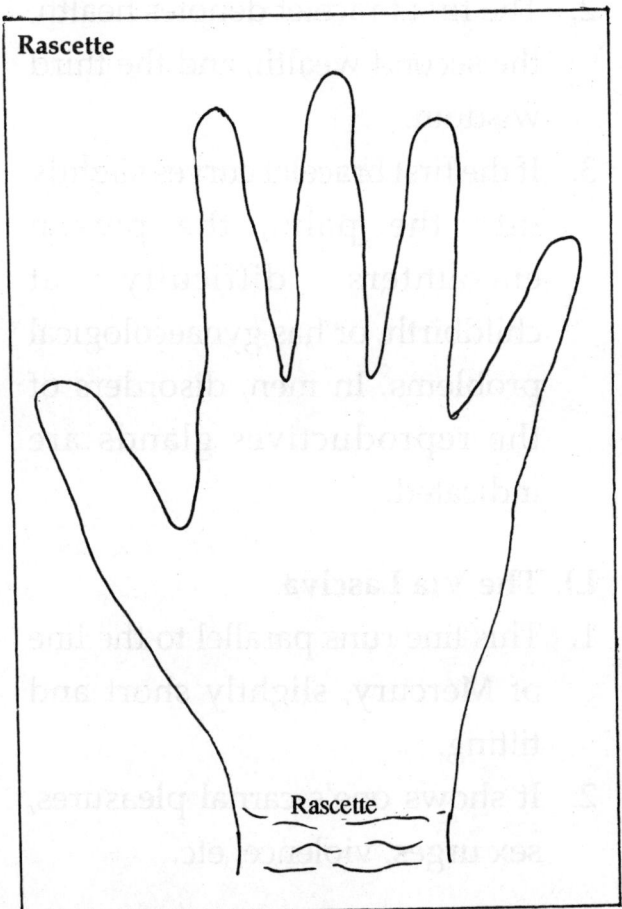

Rascette

Rascette

2. The first bracelet denotes health, the second wealth, and the third wisdom.

3. If the first bracelet curves slightly into the palm, the person encounters difficulty at childbirth, or has gynaecological problems. In men, disorders of the reproductives glands are indicated.

L) The Via Lasciva

1. This line runs parallel to the line of Mercury, slightly short and tilting.

2. It shows one's carnal pleasures, sex urges, violence, etc.

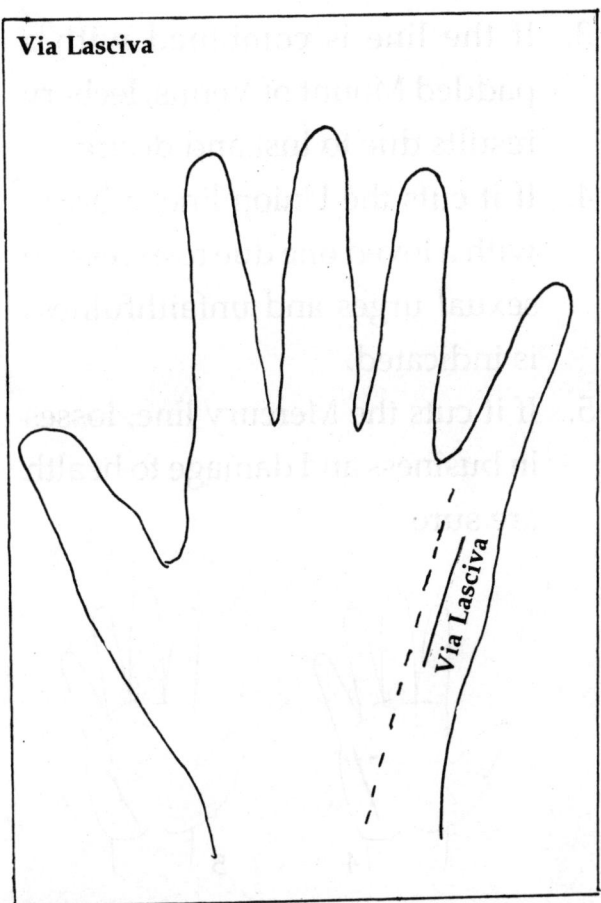

Via Lasciva

Via Lasciva

3. If the line is combined with a padded Mount of Venus, lechery results due to lust and desire.

4. If it cuts the Union line, a break with a loved one due to excessive sexual urges and unfaithfulness is indicated.

5. If it cuts the Mercury line, losses in business and damage to health are sure.

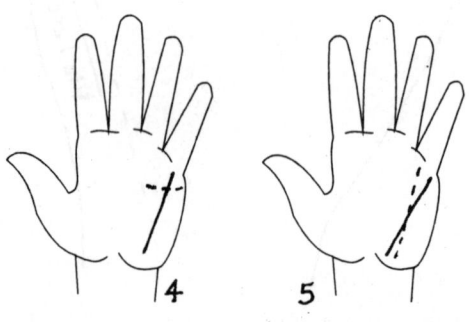

6. Combined with a clubbed thumb, it shows brutal sexual urges leading to aggression and cruelty.

M) The Bow of Intuition

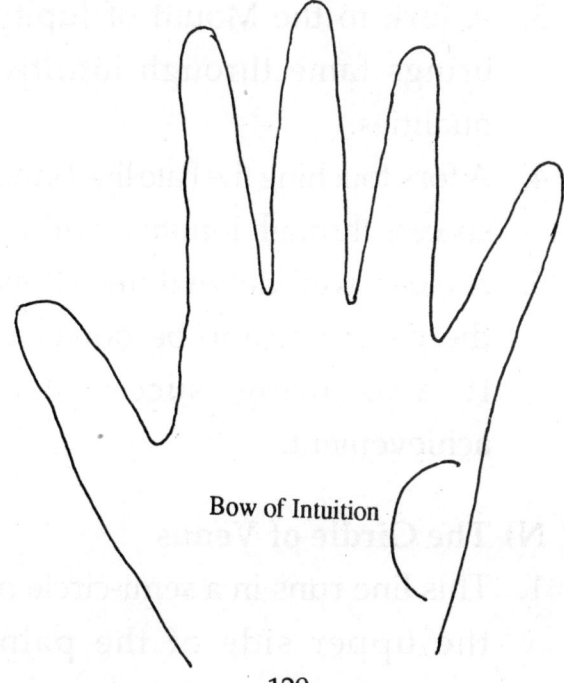

Bow of Intuition

1. This line arches between the Mount of Moon and Upper Mars.
2. It deals with our sixth sense and the ability to predict events.
3. A fork to the Mount of Jupiter brings fame through intuitive qualities.
4. A fork touching the Fate line brings success through intuitive skills.
5. A clear, well-defined line shows the inner voice to be powerful. It also bring success and achievement.

N) The Girdle of Venus
1. This line runs in a semi-circle on the upper side of the palm,

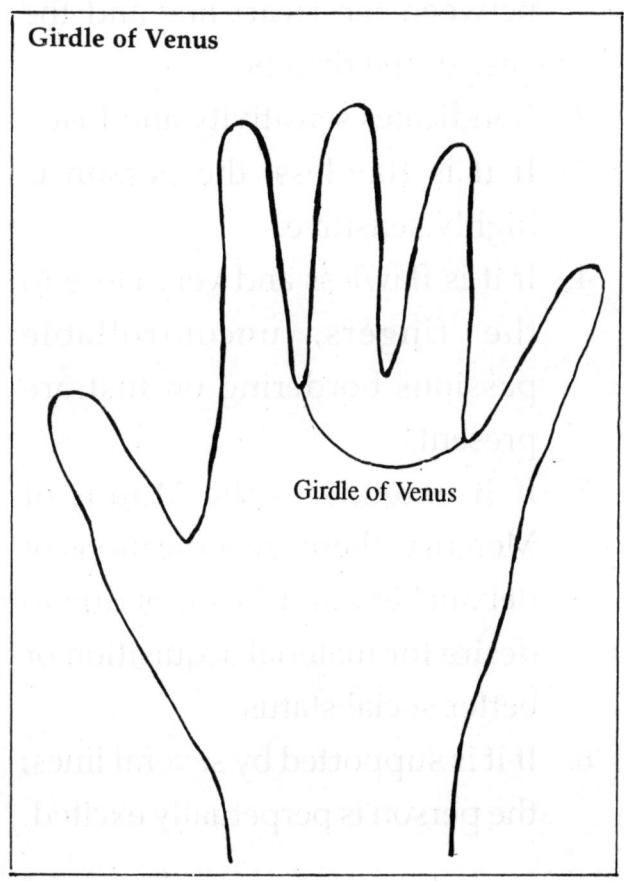

Girdle of Venus

Girdle of Venus

between the Heart line and the base of the fingers.

2. It indicates sensitivity and lust.

3. If it is flawless, the person is highly sensitive.

4. If it is flawless and very close to the fingers, uncontrollable passions bordering on lust are present.

5. If it extends to the Mount of Mercury, there are indications of debauchery and excesses due to desire for material acquisition or better social status.

6. If it is supported by several lines, the person is perpetually excited,

not easily satisfied, and lives on erotic imagination.

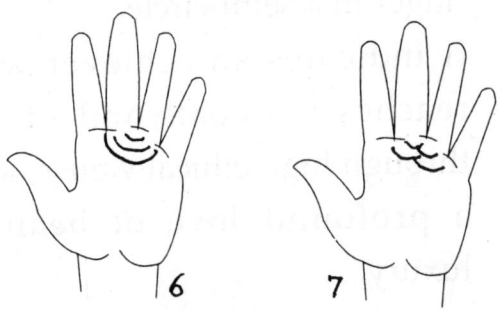

7. If it is doubled but malformed, there are perversions and promiscuity due to uncontrollable passions.
8. If it stops on the Mount of Apollo, indulgence in sexual excesses to gain success are implied.

O) The Ring of Apollo

1. This is set at the base of the ring finger in a semi-circle.
2. It indicates an achiever who reaches his goals and ideals through high ethical values, and a profound love of beauty, luxury.

P) The Ring of Solomon

1. This is set under the index finger in a curve above the Heart line.
2. It ensures knowledge, wisdom and an excellent sense of judgement.
3. The person is philosophical, and is able to benefit from experiences.

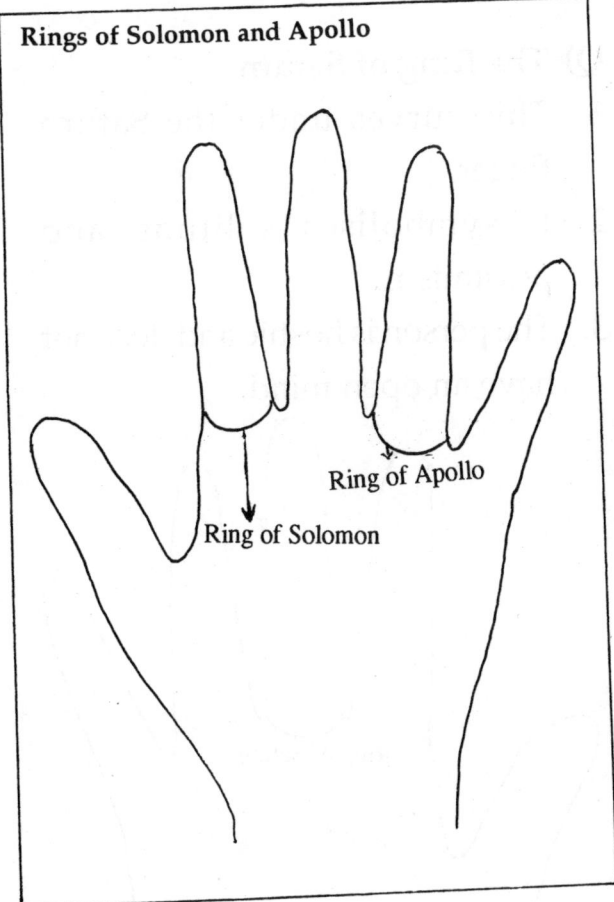

Rings of Solomon and Apollo

Ring of Apollo

Ring of Solomon

Q) The Ring of Saturn

1. This curves under the Saturn finger.

2. It symbolises solitude and pessimism.

3. The person is hostile and does not have an open mind.

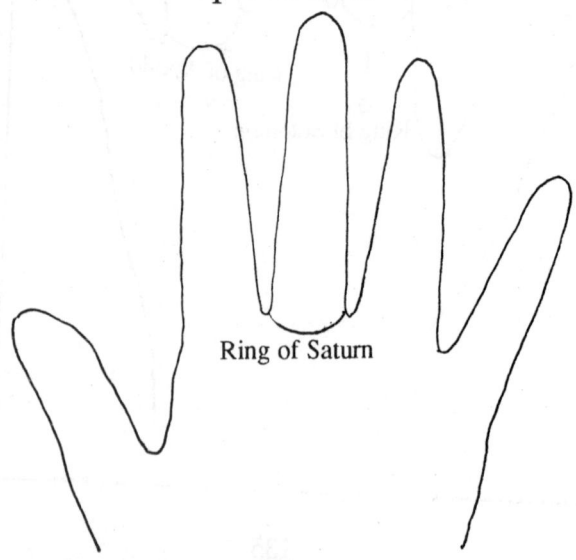

Ring of Saturn

Signs

A) A Star

1. On the Mount of Jupiter, with a good Head line—acquisition of status and honour.

2. At the base of the Mount of Jupiter—contacts with rich and influential people.

3. Along with a cross on the Mount of Jupiter—most brilliant union.

4. On the Mount of Saturn—paralysis.

5. With a square on the Mount of Saturn—escape from assassination.

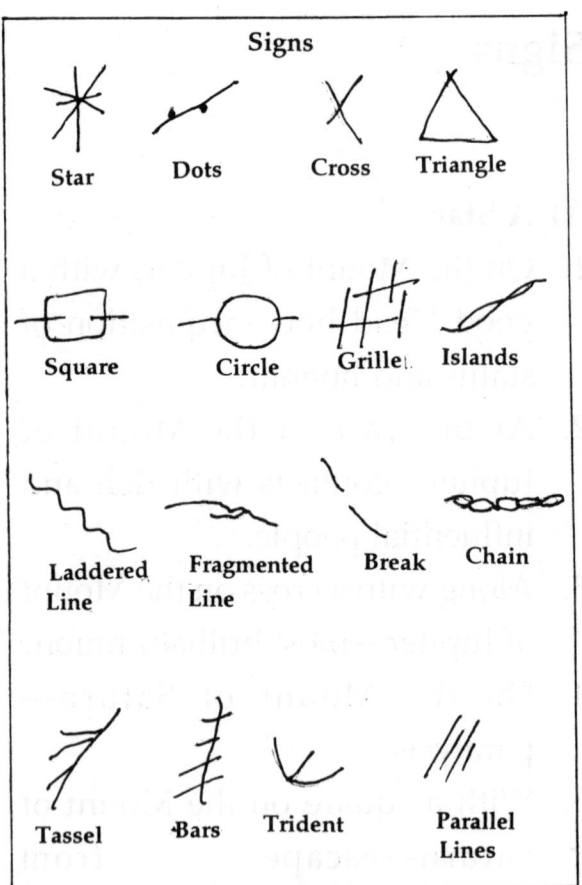

Signs

Star | Dots | Cross | Triangle

Square | Circle | Grille | Islands

Laddered Line | Fragmented Line | Break | Chain

Tassel | Bars | Trident | Parallel Lines

6. On the Mount of Mercury—dishonesty.
7. On the Mount of Moon—danger of drowning.
8. On the Lower Mars—misfortune.
9. On the Mount of Venus-death of a beloved.
10. At the base of the Mount of Venus—misfortune caused by the opposite sex.
11. In the middle of the Life line—disaster in the middle ages.
12. On the Head line—head injury.
13. On the Fate line—total distraction.
14. On the Apollo line at the end—renown and recognition.

15. At the end of the Mercury line—loss of fame and poor health.

16. Along with an island on the Mercury line—fragile health and bankruptcy.

17. At the end of the Union line—scandal.

18. On the Rascette—abundant wealth.

19. On the Bow of Intuition—clairvoyance.

B) A Dot

1. On the Mount of Jupiter—ruined reputation.

2. On the Mount of Saturn—evil possibilities.

3. On the Mount of Apollo—danger to social status.

4. On the Mount of Mercury—failure in business.

5. On the Upper Mars—a wound during a fight.

6. On the Mount of Moon—nervous trouble.

7. On the Mount of Venus—disease connected with love affairs.

8. On the Life line—stomach related ailments.

9. At the end of the Life line—death due to a head-related illness.

10. On the Heart line—disgrace, humiliation.

11. On the Head line—irritation, aggression.
12. On the Fate line—loss of reputation.
13. At the end of the Apollo line—misery in old age.
14. On the Apollo line—risk of heavy losses.
15. On the Mercury line—loss of wealth.
16. On the Union line—failure of marriage.
17. On the Via Lasciva—disgrace and humiliation.

C) A Cross

1. On the Mount of Jupiter—happy union.

2. On the Mount of Saturn—liability to accidents.

3. On the Mount of Mercury—deception.

4. On the Upper Mars—danger from fights.

5. On the Mount of Moon—a dreamy disposition.

6. On the Mount of Apollo—heavy financial losses.

7. On the Mount of Venus—a passionately erotic life

8. On the Lower Mars—withdrawal from life.

9. On the Life line—threat to life.
10. On the Head line—unhappy childhood and temporary loss of memory.
11. On the Apollo line—loss of reputation.
12. On the Rascette—grave difficulties.
13. At the end of the Bow of Intuition—fraudulence and deception .

D) A Triangle
1. On the Mount of Jupiter—a high social status and a clever diplomat.
2. On the Mount of Saturn—aptitude for the occult.

3. On the Mount of Apollo—success in art.
4. On the Mount of Mercury—scaling peaks of success.
5. On the Mount of Moon—immense creative output.
6. On the Mount of Venus—exercises charm for profit.
7. On the Mount of Mars—military skills.

E) A Square
1. On the Mount of Jupiter—social security.
2. On the Mount of Saturn—safety from danger.
3. On the Mount of Apollo—art and business.

4. On the Mount of Mercury—protection from monetary losses.
5. On the Mount of Moon—curb of an overactive imagination.
6. On the Mount of Venus—self-imposed withdrawal from worldly pleasures.
7. On the Upper Mars—a violent temper checked by reason.
8. On the Life line, on a break—protection from disaster.
9. On the Heart line—protection from emotional griefs.
10. On the Head line, on a break—a protection from disaster.
11. On the Fate line, on a break—disaster averted.

146

12. On the Apollo line—protection from loss of reputation.
13. At the end of the Apollo line—protection from losses.
14. On the Mercury line, a break—a disaster averted.
15. On a broken Union line—marriage saved.
16. On the Travel line—mishap averted.

F) A Circle
1. On the Mount of Jupiter—success.
2. On the Mount of Saturn—good omen.
3. On the Mount of Apollo—fame and fortune.

4. On the Mount of Mercury—financial collapse and death by poison.
5. On the Mount of Venus—chronic ill-health.
6. On the Life line—eye problems.
7. On the Heart line—growth of affection.
8. Many circles on the Heart line—a weak heart.
9. On the Head line—a troubled mind.
10. On the Fate line—disastrous consequences.

G) A Grille

1. On the Mount of Jupiter—loose morals.

2. On the Mount of Saturn—confusion, chaos.
3. On the Mount of Apollo—arrogance, grandular disorders.
4. On the Mount of Mercury—a violent death.
5. On the Mount of Moon—bladder problems.
6. On the Mount of Venus—prophetic dreams.
7. On the Upper Mars—danger of violent death.
8. On the Life line—betrayal by loved one.
9. On the Head line sloping to the moon—a hypochondriac.

10. On the Mercury line—losses in business.

11. On the Union line at the end—end of a relationship.

12. On the Travel line—losses during travel.

H) An Island

1. On the Mount of Jupiter—ruin caused by a friend.

2. On the Mount of Saturn—a fantastic fount of psychic knowledge.

3. On the Mount of Apollo—wasted talents.

4. On the Mount of Mercury—career prospects hampered.

5. On the Mount of Venus—unhappy marriage due to adultery.

6. On the Life line—temporary isolation.

7. On the Heart line—an affair affecting marriage and career.

8. On the Head line—depression and mental instability.

9. On the Fate line—internal conflict.

10. On the Apollo line—losses and disgrace.

11. On the Union line—misery and grief from union.

12. On the Travel line—serious consequences of a trip.

13. On the Influence line at the end—guilty of a relationship.
14. On the Bow of Intuition—sleep disorders.

I) A Laddered Line

1. On the Mount of Jupiter—a laborious rise.
2. On the Mount of Saturn—a laborious rise.
3. The Life line laddered—a hypochondriac.
4. The Mercury line laddered—business misfortunes and ill-health.

J) A Fragmented Line

1. The life line—catastrophe.
2. The Heart line—loving and losing.
3. The Head line—memory lapses.
4. The Fate line—prosperity with setbacks.
5. The Rascette—instability and insecurity.
6. The Girdle of Venus—indulgence in sexual excesses

K) Breaks in Lines

1. Life line with overlap—near escape from mishap.
2. Heart line broken under Mount of Saturn—heart-break.

3. Heart line broken under Mount of Apollo—loss of a loved one due to pride.
4. Heart line broken with a square wrapping it—a broken relationship repaired.
5. Overlapping break on the Heart line—a reunion after separation.
6. The Head line—temporary amnesia.
7. The Head line with an overlap—a head injury averted.
8. The Fate line with an overlap—a change for the better.
9. The Apollo line—a break in career

10. The Apollo line with a break in it, on the Mount of Apollo—a temporary break in the run of success.

11. The Mercury line—loss of wealth and status.

12. The Union line—a temporary breakup of a relationship.

13. The Union line with an overlap—a planned separation and later a reunion.

14. The Influence line—a temporary loss of influence.

15. The Mars line—a temporary detachment from influential people.

L) Chained Lines

1. The Life line, at the start—lethargy and prone to illness.
2. The Life line—irritability and poor health.
3. The Heart line, with chains, starting from the Mount of Saturn—dislike of the opposite sex.
4. The Head line—a chronic complainer
5. The Fate line—stumbling blocks of one's own making.
6. The Apollo line—lewd and obscene.
7. The Mercury line—pessimism, lacking foresight.

8. The Union line—selfishness.
9. The Rascette—struggle and misery.

M) A Tassel

1. The Life line, ending in a tassel—sudden exhaustion.
2. The Heart line, starting in a tassel—brief affairs, later a solid relationship.
3. The Head line, ending in a tassel—a sudden loss of memory.
4. The Apollo line, with tassel at end—wasted talents.
5. The Mercury line, ending in a tassel—negligence of health leading to a collapse.

6. The Union line, with tassel at end—an emotionless union.

N) A Bar

1. On the Mount of Saturn—loss of fame.
2. One bar on the Mount of Apollo—an excellent career and renown.
3. Two bars on the Mount of Apollo—two strong talents.
4. One bar on the Mount of Mercury—good fortune.
5. On the Upper Mars—tremendous courage.
6. Several bars on the Upper Mars—a violent temper and hostility.

7. The Life line, at the end—a unexpected death.
8. The Heart line—blockages in all fields.
9. The Apollo line, at the end—a misfortune.
10. The Apollo line—stresses and anxieties.
11. The Mercury line, ending in a bar—ruin in career and wealth.

O) A Trident

1. The Heart line, with a trident on the Mount of Jupiter—happiness.
2. The Head line ending in a trident—an excellent achiever.

3. The Fate line having a trident at the end—fantastic success.

4. The Apollo line, at the end— renown and affluence.

P) Several Parallel Lines

1. On the Mount of Jupiter— tenacity.

2. On the Mount of Saturn— pessimism.

3. On the Mount of Mercury— distinction.

4. On the Mount of Moon, confused lines—insomnia.